Rental Property Investing

How to Create Wealth and Passive Income Through Intelligent Real Estate Investing

Table of Contents

Introduction

Chapter 1: Why Rental Properties?

Chapter 2: Location Matters

Chapter 3: Which Properties Make the Best Rentals?

Chapter 4: Important Factors When Choosing a Property

Chapter 5: Your Team

Chapter 6: Making an Offer

Chapter 7: Negotiation

Chapter 8: Financing

Chapter 9: What Are the Risks Involved?

Chapter 10: How to Manage Your Properties

Chapter 11: How to Know When to Exit

Conclusion

© Copyright 2018 by _____ - All rights reserved.

The following eBook is reproduced below with the goal of providing information that is as accurate and reliable as possible. Regardless, purchasing this eBook can be seen as consent to the fact that both the publisher and the author of this book are in no way experts on the topics discussed within and that any recommendations or suggestions that are made herein are for entertainment purposes only. Professionals should be consulted as needed prior to undertaking any of the action endorsed herein.

This declaration is deemed fair and valid by both the American Bar Association and the Committee of Publishers Association and is legally binding throughout the United States.

Furthermore, the transmission, duplication or reproduction of any of the following work including specific information will be considered an illegal act irrespective of if it is done electronically or in print. This extends to creating a secondary or tertiary copy of the work or a recorded copy and is only allowed with an expressed written consent from the Publisher. All additional rights reserved.

The information in the following pages is broadly considered to be truthful and accurate account of facts, and as such any inattention, use or misuse of the information in question by the reader will render any resulting actions solely under their purview. There are no scenarios in which the publisher or the original author of this work can be in any fashion deemed liable for any hardship or damages that may befall them after undertaking information described herein.

Additionally, the information in the following pages is intended only for informational purposes and should thus be thought of as universal. As befitting its nature, it is presented without assurance regarding its prolonged validity or interim quality. Trademarks that are mentioned are done without written consent and can in no way be considered an endorsement from the trademark holder.

Introduction

Congratulations on downloading *Rental Property Investing: How to Create Wealth and Passive Income Through Intelligent Real Estate Investing* and thank you for doing so.

The following chapters will discuss everything that you could possibly want to know about investing in properties, specifically rental properties. It can seem overwhelming and as if it's only for someone with a Master's degree in business. But real estate investing is actually much simpler than you realize! It certainly helps to have the right team on your side, especially when you're not exactly sure what you're doing. Everything from an attorney to a property manager can make the process much easier and help you to earn the highest possible profit. Basically, having the right team means the difference between failing and succeeding. You'll learn why exactly rentals make the best investments, which property types are best for renting out, and why location matters so much. Your success relies on having tenants, so you need to consider what those tenants are looking for and how to provide it to them. Different properties do well in different types of locations; a multi-family home might not do as well in the city as it would in the suburbs. And while looking at potential properties can be fun, it's the business side of things that makes it a little difficult. This book helps talk you through everything necessary to help you succeed, and teaches you how to negotiate and what to do when you're ready to make an offer. And not just that, but you'll even learn about financing, and which types of loans are the best fit for you and your business. Each financing option has different pros and cons, and you'll need to figure out which one you'd prefer. And this book doesn't just talk about the benefits, but also things that could be considered negative. You'll learn about all the risks involved when investing in a rental property, and how you know when the best time to sell is. There are some really amazing tips and tricks in this book, and you'll learn so much!

There are plenty of books on this subject on the market, thanks again for choosing this one! Every effort was made to ensure it is full of as much useful information as possible. Please enjoy!

Chapter 1: Why Rental Properties?

Property investing can be confusing, expensive, and a lot of work. One of the most confusing things is that there are many different types of properties, so most people don't even know which property brings about the best profit and opportunities. Rental properties make for great investments, especially if you're a beginner.

One of the biggest reasons is that they have a lot of different finance options. You'll more than likely need to get a loan to acquire the property, and that in itself can be difficult. There is actually a loan called the "conventional loan," which is the most sought-after type of loan for rentals. As the borrower, you are required to make a down payment of around 20 to 30 percent of the full amount you take out. And that can be a lot of money upfront, but it's actually better for you in the long run. This specific type of loan has a steady and low-interest rate, which is fantastic news for a person investing in rental properties. Think about how long you'll have the property for. Typically, it's something you'd like for decades because there will always be people needing to rent, and the normal duration of a loan is around 15 to 30 years. So, having that low steady interest rate over the span of 30 years is the best possible outcome. You don't want to end up paying double the loan back, which is what can happen if your interest rate is too high. Also, a conventional loan will use your rental property as security and collateral for your loan. That means you don't have to put up your own house or car as security, which will be good if for some reason the property doesn't work out. And as an added bonus, the income you would potentially make from your rental isn't calculated into the loan. Meaning that the income you can expect to receive from your rental doesn't come into play on whether you get accepted for the loan or not. However, it's important to take the expected income into consideration so that you know whether you'd make enough to pay back the loan in time. If your income ends up being too litt e, you'll have to use other means of money to pay the loan back. You'll end up losing money over time! Make sure to calculate your potential income when deciding how much to pay back the loan each month. If a conventional loan doesn't sound like the right fit for you, you can also try a private funding loan. The negative of this type of loan is that it has a higher interest rate. On the flip side, it takes a much shorter amount of time to get this type of loan than a conventional one. Choose a private funding loan if you know that your rental investment has a really good chance of succeeding; if you have a great business plan and know the location, property, and everything else adds up perfectly for success. If you'd prefer a conventional loan, but like the quickness of a private funding loan, then you could actually get a private funding loan for a short-term need until your other conventional loan is accepted.

Rental properties have a lot of flexibility, which is another great reason to choose them! It ends up being left up to you on how you'd like to rent out your property, all while making a profit. You choose what works best for you and how to implement it. Think about it this way. There are long term and short-term type rentals. Both have negative and positive reasons to choose them, and it's up to you on what works best for you. There are the more traditional long-term rentals, which typically have a lease term of 6 to 12 months. This ensures that you are guaranteed tenants and a steady rate of occupancy, which could last for decades depending on how long the tenants would like to stay and whether they're actually good tenants. Then there are the short-term rentals, similar to how Airbnb is run. These have at most a lease term of 6 months, usually much shorter than that. They can be a little more difficult to keep up with, and you run the risk of putting up with not so great tenants. However, because it's such a short time of leasing, you're able to charge a higher income and make a bigger profit. One big benefit of having a rental property is the option of actually living there yourself. You can live in your own property, and rent out all the other space. That means instead of you paying rent, mortgage, etc., in your own house, you can make the money to pay all that through the tenants. This works best in a house or apartment that is at least 3 bedrooms and has at least 2 bathrooms. You can take up one of the bedrooms/bathrooms, and rent out the others. And it's up to you which rooms you rent out. You can decide to either take the master bedroom and rent out the smaller rooms, or take a small room and rent out the master for more money. Doing this also has the added bonus of a more convenient financing options since it's easier to finance your main home residence.

Rental property investing is a very low risk, which is why it's such a good choice for beginners. You can learn all you need to know about the process of investing in rentals, and either keep up with them or move on to bigger properties. You go through the entire process of buying a rental, looking it over, adding up the various expenses, and learning how to manage it, all without worrying about a high risk. Of course, as a beginner, you'll definitely make mistakes and deal with many issues. But since rental properties tend to have a slightly higher turn around rate, you'll be able to learn from those mistakes and fix them for the future. You'll only make a mistake once, so eventually, you reach that optimal level of success. Plus, doing all the work yourself means you'll be able to understand what goes into managing a property. Which means, at the point when you're financially able to hire someone to manage it for you, you'll still be able to understand what's going on in your property and won't be taken advantage of.

When making investments, thinking about the long run is always a good idea. You want something that will last for a very long time, and bring in a steady income. Something that can keep bringing in money even past the typical "retirement" age. And that's where rental properties come in. They have the most to offer in the tumultuous world of real estate. They have a big enough profit that all the costs you've made for the investment are covered, and they bring in an income and a good investment return that lasts many years. Long enough, in fact, that you can pay off the loan and make a profit. You even have the option to sell eventually, getting all your money back plus extra. It means being patient of course. This isn't the type of investment that will earn you quick money. But you'll be earning a great income if you can think in the long term. And not just a normal income, but passive income which is the best type. You can go about your life, doing other work if you want, all while earning profit. A rental doesn't take up too much of your time, so having just one or two can be a great way to earn some passive income with it not taking up too much of your time.

Chapter 2: Location Matters

Location is probably the most important thing when figuring out which property you'd like to invest in. After all, your future tenants will want an area that best suits their needs, and one they can call home for many years to come. That means that not only do you need to check out the property and its neighbors, but also the surrounding area. How many grocery stores there are, whether it's walkable or not, nearby gas stations, what kind of restaurants are around it, etc. You have to think about who you want to rent to and find the best location that caters to that type of person. If you'd prefer renting to young professionals, then a city-type area with hip restaurants, local attractions, and organic grocery stores makes more sense than an area in the suburbs with a lot of kid-friendly attractions. The reverse is true as well; if you know your tenants will most like be families, then choosing a property in a good school district makes more sense than one being next door to a hip bar. And it's not just the local attractions that you have to consider. Think about where exactly your property is sitting. Is it on a spacious street with good lighting and lots of street parking, or is the only entrance down a dark alley? Families prefer good yards and lots of safe outdoor space, so a multi-family home on a cul-de-sac will rent much better than one on a busy street. You might be able to find a great fixer-upper for pretty cheap, but if no one rents it because of the location, then it'll end up just costing you much more than you'd want.

Keep in mind that location is really the only permanent thing about your property. You can change the wall colors, change the furniture, even rebuild completely! But you're always going to be in that specific location, so make sure it's one that you'd like to stay with for many years to come. In fact, keep an eye out on future trends and up and coming neighborhoods. If you know that a neighborhood is not so great now, but there are plans to rebuild and revitalize it in the next few years, you could buy a property there for very cheap and fix it up. Once you're ready to rent it out, the neighborhood will be much better, and people will be more willing to live in a cool and hip area. This will also help a lot if you end up selling. You could potentially make a very good profit! Just be careful because there could be ideas thrown around to fix the neighborhood up, but nothing actually happens. Look around at what other kinds of businesses there are, and if there are condos and cafes popping up.

Where the property is geographically located is pretty important. There's such a thing as supply and demand, even in real estate. It's best to look around the area and see how many properties there are for rent. You don't want to be number 40 on a very long list; that's just too many, and the area is saturated with available properties. The fact that there's so many is a big indication that something's wrong with the neighborhood. Maybe the crime rate is high, or it floods every time it rains. Whatever the reason, if potential tenants see so many properties available, they'll think something is wrong and look elsewhere. You also need to look in an area that actually has a lot of people in it. If you think the idea of investing in a property in a small town is "quaint," think again! You should be in a location that actually has a good supply; supply being possible tenants. It's best to find a happy medium. Look for properties in an area that has a few for rent, but not too many, with many people for lots of options.

Location also matters when you consider who exactly you're renting to. You obviously want a location that has access to great amenities like internet, etc., but what about public transportation? Many people who live in a city don't have a car or only use their car very rarely. So, a property that has easy access to the local bus route or train will be in higher demand than one that requires a long walk just to get to the bus. What kind of amenities that are around your property depends on whether you're looking to rent to long term or short-term tenants. Those looking to stay for a long time would prefer to be close to schools, hospitals, grocery stores, etc. However, short-term tenants, like Airbnb guests, typically prefer the more touristy stuff. They would need good access to public transportation, restaurants, and easy access to activities. While garage parking would be important for long-term rentals, short-term tenants probably wouldn't care as much. The first thing to do is figure out who you'd rather rent to, and choose the best location off that. Remember though that both long and short-term tenants want to be in safe areas with good utilities.

Speaking more about short-term tenants, keep in mind that you might not be able to do traditional rentals. A multi-family house in the suburbs would be great for long-term tenants, but most Airbnb guests would prefer to stay closer to the city. They would be fine with smaller rooms and not every amenity (depending on the length of stay). Many tourists visit to see the city and all it has to offer, so they're more willing to overlook things that long-term tenants would prefer to have in their house.

Location is also important to how much of a profit you'll make. Different areas mean different costs, and what you could charge for rent in one location could be way too expensive for another. Research other properties in the area, similar to the one you're looking to invest in. See how much they're costing, and how much other property holders are charging. It's important to also keep track of how much it will cost you every month to run the property. Some months will be cheaper than others, but sometimes you'll have something unexpected come up. You don't need to replace the water heater every year, but adding it to your expenses will help you to know how much exactly your property will cost you over the years. A property that looks amazing has all the latest upgrades, and a beautiful yard will rent much better in an area with other similar properties. On the flip side, if you have an older property that is livable but runs down, you'll only be able to charge so much for it. Especially in an area that has very beautiful and modern homes. If the upgraded home next door rents for $1400 a month, and your property is about worth half that, then you'd only be able to charge your tenants $700 a month. Which is good news for them, but you'll end up paying a lot out of pocket. Whereas if the older property is in a neighborhood with other older homes, and the one next door is $1400, then you'd be able to charge the same amount.

You really have to think about location long-term when investing in rental properties. And not just about the property, but the land itself. If you choose one that is in a very good location, with high demand, then you can make a very good profit down the road. This is known as real estate appreciation, and it considers how valuable land is, and how much more valuable it will be in the future. If there is a neighborhood being built by a lot of empty land, then it's pretty much guaranteed that the land next to it will also have homes in the next few years. If you invest in one of those first homes, before the area really starts to boom, then you'll be able to make a great profit later on down the road. Once a neighborhood is built, people will want amenities. Which means restaurants, grocery stores, malls, and movie theaters. And once those are built, many more people will want to move to the area. By buying ahead of the curve, you'll already have real estate available for those looking to rent. You'll be able to up the rental rate once more things become available around your property, which means you'll be making a bigger profit. And eventually, you can even sell if you'd prefer. What about a location that's next to many businesses? Maybe you've stumbled on a home for sale in an area where new restaurants, pharmacies, and stores are popping up. If you invest in the right property, the land might end up being worth more than the house. You can rent out the property for as long as you'd like, and sell once you've been approached by a big business.

Another thing to consider when looking at locations are the local laws. Eviction laws can be a pain and end up having a negative effect on you and your property. Obviously, you don't want to actually go through the process of evicting someone, but sometimes it's a necessary evil. If you have a tenant not paying rent, then the legal thing to do is evict them. However, in some states, it can actually take months to legally evict a person, which means they can technically stay on your property and not pay. You end up losing months of money waiting around for the law. And what about changing the rent? Sometimes the property value goes up, and your rent needs to keep up with the area. However, some places have what is called rent stabilization laws, which means you might not be able to actually raise the rent however you like. And what about their security deposit? Most tenants take pretty good care of the property they're renting, but sometimes you end up with ones that trash your place. Or even accidentally damage something. That's where their security deposit comes in. Typically, you use that to pay for whatever damage they inflict, accidentally or otherwise. But if it comes into question, some states will side with the tenant no matter what. It's best to find out which areas are the most landlord friendly, and figure out a location based on that.

Chapter 3: Which Properties Make the Best Rentals?

We all know that mistakes happen; accidentally saying the wrong thing, bumping into someone, or dropping what you were just holding. But while these mistakes are pretty small and can be overlooked, choosing the wrong rental property can really mess up your new real estate company. It can mean a lot of unnecessary stress, be very expensive to fix, and even cause you yourself to feel ill. So how do you make sure to choose the best property? There's so many out there, and there's a lot of different questions you can ask yourself to help.

What to buy, what to not buy, how many bedrooms, should the property have a garage, what are the neighbors like, what's the color of the property, how old is it, how big is it. Keeping these basic questions in mind will help you to find the best property for your business.

Multi-Family Homes: The ultimate goal is to find long-term tenants, which is hard to do with single family homes, depending on the family. When there are only one or two bedrooms, tenants might stay for a year or two but eventually move out. Think about it - people usually end up getting married and having kids and need a lot of space for their future plans. By choosing three or four-bedroom houses for your rentals, you're ensuring that your tenants will stay for at least 5 years! And if you ever get to the point of needing to sell, three to four-bedroom houses sell best because, again, of all those families looking for the perfect home.

Single-Family Homes: These homes probably make the next best rentals. They're the easiest to manage, mainly because those renting them tend to treat these types of houses as if they are their own homes. While some people like living in apartments, most would prefer a house with a yard. However, most people also don't want too big of a house or to buy a house outright, which is why they're renting. It's possible for you to find tenants that would prefer to stay renting a single-family home for decades, which would definitely benefit you. Since the renters see the home as theirs, they also usually do some of the repairs needed and take better care of the yard. And unlike apartments, in single-family homes, the tenant pays all of the utilities, which makes it much easier for you.

Apartment: Two-bedroom apartments are actually pretty good, and liked by a lot of people. People seem to be moving slightly away from the suburban life, and wanting to live closer to the city. It can be difficult for families because it's hard to find a two or three-bedroom house in a city. So many families compromise and look for a two-bedroom apartment. The type of person can affect your rental business too; you want to rent to a professional, someone you know that will be able to afford your rent. And typically, a professional single person prefers a two-bedroom apartment over a studio or one bedroom. It's extra space for their office or a work out room. Studios and one-bedroom apartments usually have a high turnover in their tenants, even with a 12-month contract. So, renting out a two-bedroom apartment is a good middle ground for someone looking to rent a place for a few years. You can try investing in and renting out a one bedroom or studio apartments, but you run the risk of a high turnover rate. Of course, it's possible to find a single person that is professional and wants to stay in the apartment long term, but the norm is typically the opposite. If you're looking for the best possible chance to make a profit with an apartment, then a two bedroom makes the most sense.

Chapter 4: Important Factors When Choosing a Property

Just like there are types of properties that make for fantastic rentals, there are ones that really aren't great and tend to cost you more in the long run. You really don't want to be putting in more money than you're making; eventually, you'll either lose a bunch of money or go out of business, and both of those scenarios are terrible ones! There are several things you can consider when choosing the right property, and several things to keep an eye out for that you'll know to stay away from. Of course, an important thing to remember are the different trends and fads in your current location. While choosing to invest in a studio apartment might seem like not a great idea, if your location is primarily in a city then having a few smaller apartments to rent out would make sense. Here's a list of things to consider when looking for ideal properties:

Bedrooms: Bedrooms are always top of the list when looking at properties. The number of bedrooms caters to different types of tenants, and it all depends on who you'd like to rent to. You also have to think of whether you'd like to sell or not. Studio and one-bedroom apartments usually have a higher turn around rental time, so if you're looking for long term tenants then stay away from those type of properties. Sometimes more bedrooms can cause issues too. If you have too many rooms, then typically your tenants will be ones with a lot of children. Which isn't necessarily a bad thing, but kids can cause a lot of wear and tear to a property. You have to think about how kids can break, tear, and stain, and decide whether it's worth it. If you do try renting out a house with many bedrooms, make sure you have an iron-clad security deposit!

Age: Older homes can be a lot more expensive to fix. You can probably buy one for pretty cheap, which is great, but you also have to think about how much it'll cost to actually fix it. You could end up spending more in the long run on an older home than the upfront costs of a newer one. A simple project could end up being a lot more hassle than originally thought, and it's entirely possible that the previous work done on it over the years wasn't up to standard and code. Energy costs will be higher in an older property as well. You can get around that by having the tenants pay their own utility bills, but if they actually figure it out, then you'll end up having a higher turnover rate in renters. To bypass all this stress, you could simply just invest in newer homes.

Garage: Homes without a garage don't usually stay rented for long periods of times. Think about where you're located and what the weather is like. Does it rain or snow a lot? Weather can cause a lot of wear and tear to a person's car, and end up costing the tenant money. Even hot days can make it unbearable, especially if your tenant has leather seats! Plus, having lots of storage is really nice. If you're investing in single family homes, there might not be a lot of storage. So, having a garage can really help sell your property. If you're looking for long-term tenants, then it's best to stay away from homes without garages.

Utilities: While most renters don't like paying for utilities separate from their rent, it's actually an ideal situation for you. Having the tenants pay their own utility bills is definitely a better situation to be in for you. Think about it like this - if your tenant doesn't have to worry about utilities, they'll probably leave the AC running all the time, especially during summer. Maybe there's a small drip in the faucet; they don't mention it because they're not paying for it, and it ends up costing an extra few hundred dollars a year. So, it's definitely recommended to stay away from properties that have all the bills being paid for by you the owner. That can be a little more difficult in multi-family homes, so try to find ones that at least have electricity and heat being paid for by the renter. It's possible to have them pay the water as well, through a system called master metered. Your renters are able to pay their own water bill through it, which will help you immensely.

Lawn: Stay away from properties with large yards! Tenants won't expect to take care of the yard of a property they're renting, which means it'll be up to you. So, either you'll have to spend your own time and money keeping up with the yard, hire someone to do it which will cost money, or make the tenant do it which they won't be too happy about. On the flip side, if you're renting out a multi-family home, it's important for most families to have a yard that their kids can run around in. Many people like having a space for recreation, planting, or backyard bar-b-que's, so your best option is finding homes that have yards but in a smaller scale. Keep in mind other outdoor features too. Do you really want to deal with the upkeep of a fountain? What about a pool in the backyard? Pool maintenance can be difficult and expensive, and it will most likely be up to you as the landlord to keep up with. If something breaks or malfunctions, the tenant will expect you to fix it in a timely manner. Instead of all that stress and hassle, invest in properties that don't even have all that extra stuff.

Parking: Tenants love a good parking spot! Some places have enough room for just one vehicle, which will deter most people. Even if you're renting to only one person, they could have visitors over who then wouldn't have anywhere to park. Parking off the street is something most tenants prefer as well, so stay away from properties that don't have adequate parking. Look for covered or garages, and try to find more than one parking spot.

Location: Location is probably one of the most important factors when looking at a property. People want to live in an area they love, and one that they'll want to actually be in. They'll want to visit local restaurants, walk around, be by their favorite grocery store. If they have children, they'll want to be in the right school district or close to a good daycare. And for many people, a shorter commute is definitely ideal. Of course, tenants will want to be in a safe neighborhood as well, so it's best to look for properties in an area with a low crime rate. If you're in the middle of the city with lots of cafes, restaurants, and boutiques, then it makes sense to look for properties that cater to a more "hip" crowd. Most families tend to be in actual neighborhoods or suburbs, so investing in a large multi-family home in the middle of a city doesn't really make sense. The opposite of that also applies. If you're looking to invest in properties in more of a suburb-like setting, then choosing a studio or one-bedroom apartments wouldn't be a good financial decision.

Number of Tenants: How many tenants you'd like to rent to will definitely factor into the properties you're looking at. Typically, it's one person to a bedroom unless your tenants are a couple. There are a few exceptions though. If you're looking near a college, it might make sense to invest in a large house with many bedrooms. More than five if you can wing it! Doing it this way means that instead of renting to one or two students, you would be able to rent out the home to multiple students. Of course, keep in mind that the more tenants than, the more wear and tear you'll have on the property. But this is where location comes into play. By investing in a multi-family home near a college, you're ensured that there will always be students looking for a place to rent. The turn-over might be high; most students graduate within four years. But the college will always be there, so there will always be students. If you'd only like to have just a few tenants, then it makes more sense to go after the smaller properties. Renting out a 5-bedroom house to only 2 people can mean that you lose money on maintenance and utility costs. It's a large space, one that would need expensive fixing up if something happens, and having the rent of just two tenants probably wouldn't cover the issue.

Chapter 5: Your Team

There's a lot that goes into investing in real estate, especially rental properties. You can try to take on everything, but you'll find yourself getting overwhelmed pretty quickly. Things will be much easier if you build a team, one that you can rely on for many years to come. It's possible if you're buying just one small property, then you could potentially do everything yourself. But honestly, that sounds like bankruptcy just waiting to happen! Because it's not just a property manager that would be helpful, but someone to take care of all the legalities and information you just don't know much about.

Real Estate Agent: A real estate agent is going to become your best friend. You'll need someone that knows all about short sales, foreclosures, and how to broker. Because chances are that those are the types of properties, you'll end up investing in.

Accountant: You'll want to make sure your business is set up legally, and that's something an accountant can help with. You also don't want to have to worry about taxes and everything that goes into it. Not only can taxes be confusing for a business, but if you mess up then you might get audited by the IRS and possible owe a lot of money.

Attorney: Another person you absolutely need to have on your team is an attorney. They can help with all the necessary paperwork and contracts, which you'll be writing a lot of. You'll need contracts between you and the tenants, between you and your loan people, and between you and anyone else you end up working with. One small mistake in a contract can mean you end up losing money and possibly even your property. Contracts are also very important if you end up being taken to court. Let's say you have a contract between you and your tenant. You put in there that it's a 12-month contract, which means after 12 months everything in there needs to be renegotiated, including the rent payment. During the 12 months you have in there that the rent stays as is, but once the lease term is up, then you can raise the rent due to property taxes, etc. So, in the new contract, you put in there that rent has been raised by just $20, which the tenant agrees to. They sign the contract, and now have the obligation to pay their original rent, plus $20. But instead of doing that, they keep paying what they originally paid. You're owed that money, but you're not getting it. Because of them signing the contract, you're able to take them to court (if necessary), and they're legally required to pay you what you're owed. If you didn't have that contract, then you never would've been paid that money. An attorney can help make sure your contracts are worded in your favor and with any court proceedings if you need them.

Property Inspector: You need to know the condition of the home you're interested in investing in, whether it's a good deal or just not worth it. A good property inspector can help you to understand everything that's needed to make the potential home worth renting out. The property could look perfectly fine, but an inspector does more than just look at the cosmetic value. They look into the wiring, plumbing, the roof condition, the condition of the insulation, and even the structural integrity. They look over everything and helps you to know exactly how much of an investment you'd need to make. Having one on your team is definitely a benefit to you and to them. You can keep using the same inspector for each property, especially if you know they're very thorough and take their job seriously. If you're insistent on buying a property that might have some big money issues, your inspector can tell you exactly how much it would cost to fix them. You can then take that number to the sellers and renegotiate the selling price. A property inspector can actually save you a lot of money and hassle in the long run.

Mortgage Lender: You really want a great mortgage lender on your team. Someone who asks you questions knows their industry and provides you with several options to meet your specific needs. It's up to you to be responsible for each document you're signing and having a mortgage lender who actually takes the time to explain them to you will definitely benefit you. They can help you with any issues that come up and work with you if anything happens to your current mortgage program. You need one who stays in touch and makes sure that you close on your loan in a timely manner. It's entirely possible to end up losing a lot of money because of a bad mortgage lender, so make sure you find one that is really good.

Estate Attorney: Different from a real estate attorney, an estate attorney is someone who helps you specifically and not your business. They can still give you great advice, but they are there to help draft your will and plan what happens to your estate once you're gone. It can be a difficult thing to think about at the best of times, but it's especially difficult if you have a lot of properties. What happens to those properties once you move on? Who do they go to? You need to decide if they are getting passed on to a specific family member or just leave them for the bank. Keep in mind that it's not just you that you need to think of though. You probably have a lot of tenants, who rely on you for their housing needs. So, once you're gone and the properties are no longer in your control, what happens to them? That's where an estate attorney comes in. You can work together to draft a will that takes care of all your tenants, and whether they can stay at your properties for a certain amount of time, etc. You definitely don't want everyone evicted just because you're no longer around!

Property Manager: You might start out with just one or two properties, and be able to handle it all on your own. But at some point, you'll start becoming overwhelmed and not sure how to handle everything thrown at you. And that's when you bring in a property manager. It's all in the name - they are someone who is there specifically to manage your properties, so you don't have to. They deal with all the little issues that pop up, things that you really shouldn't have to figure out yourself. Maybe one of the tenants is blaring music at 3 in the morning. Is that something you really want to deal with? Instead, unleash your property manager and let them handle it! And while they're technically your employee and you're paying them to do all this, they also need to be someone you can work closely with and trust implicitly.

The Rest: There's a ton of others that you can have on your team, but many are optional and completely up to you. If your properties have a yard, then you'll need a good landscaping company. Maybe you hire someone to come in and clean once a week; obviously not the tenants living quarters, but the hallways and entrance. You could even hire someone to decorate for you, which would make the property a lot more appealing to potential renters.

Whoever you have on your team, and whether it ends up being just one person or ten, they need to be people you can really put your trust in. People who you know will help you succeed, and people you can keep on your team for many years to come. Having the right team makes all the difference when it comes to failing or succeeding, and they will help you to become the best you can be in your business.

Chapter 6: Making an Offer

Making an offer can seem like a scary thing. You've come up with a realistic price for your budget, you've considered whether it's a seller's or buyer's market, and you've done all the research needed. All that's left is to send the offer over, but that in itself can be difficult. Once you've put the offer in then, you're legally obligated to follow through. Just knowing that can make you feel nervous or unsure if you're making the right decision and whether it's one you're ok to see through. Luckily, having a real estate agent can help with the fine print. They know what to put in an official offer to make sure you, as the buyer, are protected. A basic offer is one that says you're willing to buy the property at this price, but only if the loan and conditions you prefer are met. However, it's not just the one clause that can help you, but a few other things you need to take into consideration.

View the Interior: It's important to look at the inside of the property you want to invest in. You have to know what you're getting into, and the only way to do that is by actually looking at the interior of the property. Some sellers might be finicky about it, so make sure to actually put in your offer clause that the offer is only viable if you're satisfied and approve of all the interiors in the property. The first inspection is probably the most important thing to do, before anything else just in case if you don't actually like the property and decide to not invest in it.

Numbers: It's very important that all the numbers add up before making an offer. And not just the final price of everything added up, but all the itemized things too. Look at all the statements involving income and expenses, and see if everything adds up to the expected price. For example, if the expense statement includes material costs because the owner happens to be doing the repairs himself, then renegotiate. It's not on you to pay for his repairs unless it's something you're willing to compromise on.

Taxes: Look at the tax information on the property, and make sure what the seller has been reporting adds up. You should be looking at the past few years to ensure a thorough investigation. Maybe the rent income has been pretty steady over the years but recently has become a lot higher. It's possible that's just to try and sell the property at a higher rate. By looking at the previous statements, you can see for yourself if the value is correct or not. Looking at the previous tax statements are good in general, just to make sure that the numbers are lining up.

Hiring a real estate broker to help you negotiate the offer can be very helpful and will greatly benefit you. You can try to do it yourself of course, but having that extra help is nice, and they might catch things that you don't.

Chapter 7: Negotiation

Negotiation will become your best friend. It's something you should learn inside and out because everything is negotiable, especially in real estate. There are so many things you can negotiate on - the final price of the property you're interested in, what conditions you want for the payment, how long of a payment period you'd like, how much you're renting it out for, even the furniture and various objects that can come with the property. You definitely want the best deal possible, once that leaves you feeling satisfied and proud of yourself when investing in a property. However, negotiation is a skill, one that you'll get better with as time goes on. You'll learn the various tips and tricks, and what works for you and what doesn't. It can be difficult when you're just starting out, but as you get more experience in real estate investing, you'll also get more experienced in negotiating. Here are some specific tricks you can keep in mind to help you be the best possible negotiator:

Finances: You definitely don't want to spend more than you can afford, and sometimes that happens when you're negotiating. Maybe you've gotten caught up in the process and excitement, and think that spending a few extra thousand won't hurt. But then you go back afterwards and realize you actually can't afford what you originally agreed to. Which means you either have to renegotiate or cancel the contract completely. This will cause you to lose money and whomever you're negotiating with probably won't work with you again. Either of these can have very negative effects on your business. The best thing to do? Figure out your finances before going into the negotiation. Look at how much cash you have available and any other means of money. Make a budget, and see how much potential spending you'd do for the property, how much money you have available at this exact moment, and how much of a profit you'd expect to make. You need to be profitable from the very first month or else your business can easily fail. Once you've put together your budget, you know the exact number you can't go over when negotiating. You're going to come across properties that you'd love to invest in but just can't quite afford yet. And while it'll be difficult, you might just have to walk away. Focus on the properties you can afford, and go back to the more expensive ones later, once you can realistically afford them.

Analyze: After figuring out the property you want to invest in, and once you're ready to move forward, the best step you can take is doing an analysis of the real estate market in the area. You need to figure out what the surrounding properties are going for or how much they've sold for in the past few weeks/months. Look at the selling prices, not the asking prices. The selling prices are a better example of what your new property is worth and how much you can realistically expect to ask for when negotiating. Keep that number in mind when going throughout the negotiating process and be firm!

Identify: You need to figure out if you're working in a buyer's or seller's market. One is obviously better for you, but you can still be successful in negotiations if you know ahead of time which market is trending at the moment. To know for sure, look at how many properties are listed in your area, how long they've been on the market, how much they're going for, the difference in listing and selling price, and the closing percentage. There's a big difference when investing in a property if it's a buyer's market. You're able to take a lot more time before you actually close on the deal, you have the opportunity to counter with a lower price than is originally asked, and you can even ask for some things that would be a lot more beneficial to you (like the owner leaving furniture, doing extra repairs, etc.). On the opposite side, however, things are a lot different when it's a seller's market. You need to act quickly, be prepared to pay a higher price than originally asked, offer conditions that are more beneficial to the previous owner, and remember to not expect a lot to come with the property. What makes things a lot more difficult is that competition is much more fierce with other buyers, so you have to act quickly and won't be able to bargain when doing negotiations.

Real Estate Agent: Although you might not want to spend the upfront costs of hiring a real estate agent, it's definitely worth it if you want the best deal possible. This is even more pertinent if you're a newbie, and don't really know what you're doing. A real estate agent can make the negotiation process run smoothly and takes over the negotiations completely. Some people tend to be more introverted too, so if you don't want to deal with negotiations or speaking to the seller directly, then a real estate agent makes sense! Plus, an agent is much less likely to make a mistake if you're just starting out. You can learn from them and once you know more, then try the negotiations yourself.

The Why: Why is the seller selling? It's best to know the reasons before negotiating because it will give you leverage going in. Maybe they just want to be closer to family, or maybe there's something seriously wrong with the property. If it's the latter, then you can renegotiate the selling price to go way down, which would be in your favor. And knowing why they're selling helps you to know when to press harder in your negotiations and when to back down.

Negotiate, Negotiate, Negotiate: When investing in real estate, the key to getting the best possible deal and benefiting your business is to remember that you can negotiate everything, not just the price. You can try to negotiate the closing costs and date, the warranties, repairs, if the owner can leave any of the appliances or furniture, etc. Basically everything! It's especially helpful if the market is trending at a seller's market and you might not get the exact price you wanted. Instead, you can try for a deal that everyone's happy with by getting different types of benefits. Investing in rental property is all about the long term, so those extra benefits might end up putting a higher value on your property. If you decide to sell, you could end up getting a great little profit.

Compromise: It can be hard to compromise, especially if you've had your heart set on a certain price and if you tend to lean towards the stubborn side. You want to negotiate in a way where everyone ends up happy, not just you. Look at the surrounding homes that have sold recently, and negotiate the price to reflect that. For example, let's say a home nearby sold for $600,000, and it doesn't have any add-ons, like a pool, fireplace, etc. But the property you're looking at investing in has all that, plus more. So it's really not a smart business decision to try and buy that property for less than $600,000; there's no way the seller will want to sell it at that price or even negotiate. They'll just move on to the next buyer and pass you up. And if you've found a property that you really like, then don't pay more than you're willing to actually pay. While it's important to make sure the seller is happy, you need to compromise for yourself too. If you just can't reach a good price for both you and the seller, then remember it's ok to walk away. This isn't going to be your home, it's your business. And you need to make decisions that are good for your business and make sense specifically from an investor's viewpoint.

Chapter 8: Financing

Unless you have tons of extra cash laying around, you're going to need some financial help when investing in properties. It can seem overwhelming and difficult, especially if you've never gotten financing help before. As long as you have fairly good credit and a decent income, then you shouldn't have any issues borrowing money from lenders. You have a few different options to choose from:

Owner Occupant (OO): This one has very specific terms that you need to follow, but it can actually be the best option. Basically, you choose the property you'd like to buy as your rental. But instead of buying it as a business, you purchase it as a personal residence. This means you live there for the next 12 months, which is a requirement for an owner occupant loan. By doing this, you can actually get the best possible financing terms, interest rate, and down payment. After the 12 months, the loan still has the same terms from when you first signed up, but you're able to move and rent it out. You can keep living in it of course, but that option to move out is still there. A great reason for this option is the fact that you're living in this property for a whole year. You get to learn about any issues popping up and anything that needs to be fixed, and actually, have the time to do it before renting it out. Plus, if there is something that needs to be done, like any renovations, then you can do them without spending a ton of money. If you were in your own house and had to make renovations to your rental property, that would mean you'd be making double payments on two homes. That's a lot of money all at once! And as an added bonus, you'll end up being a lot more selective in the type of property you purchase. You'll invest in something that you yourself would want to live in, which means it'll probably be a higher quality than something you wouldn't stay in. The higher quality of home means higher quality of tenant. A great thing about this type of loan is that you can keep doing it over and over again. The loan terms run in yearly increments, so you can either choose 12 months, 24 months, or 36 months. Once the term is over, you can move out. When you know it's getting time to move out, then just buy another property with another owner-occupant loan and move into that one. You'll be able to rent out the first property and live in the second. Then when the term is up for the second one, you can buy a third and start the process over. You'll end up with however many homes you'd like to make rental properties, and end up making some great profits.

Straight Rental Property: Another option is buying it as a straight rental property. To go this route, you'd need a large down payment, which is why many choose the owner occupancy loan. But for those who can afford it, doing it this way means you'll be able to rent the property out pretty much right away instead of waiting one to three years. The down payment is typically 20 to 25 percent for many of the lenders, although you could possibly find some for 10 percent. But you also have to consider any extra costs, like closing and renovation. So actually, you'd need about 30 to 35 percent upfront. And for a $150,000 property, that would be $50,000 cash, upfront and all at once. In addition to that, you'd also need to make sure you have good credit and actually qualify for the lenders financing program. Of course, there are some pretty good benefits to this type of loan with rental properties. Many banks include an estimate of the net rental income, which can help your debt to income. And a lot of times rental properties can already have tenants in place, which will be very advantageous to you. If the tenants are at the rental already, you can actually get the security deposit from the person selling during closing, and even some of the pro-rated rent. Your mortgage payment is typically due a month after everything is done, so you'll be able to collect that first month's rent before having to start your mortgage payments. Plus, you're also able to make your mortgage payment due on a specific date, so you can make it after rent is due. That way, you'll get all the rent payments before having to pay your mortgage payment. Of course, there's also the added benefit of there being no vacancy, so you don't have to go through the hassle of trying to find tenants. It can be a huge pain finding someone trustworthy to rent your property, so already having people there makes things so much easier. And since there are already people living there, you probably won't have to make any renovations until after they leave. That saves hugely on the costs, and you're able to spread out what you'd be spending total on the property. There are negatives to having tenants already living in your new rental property though. You could have someone who doesn't pay on time, pays too low of a rental rate for the market, someone who just doesn't pay, or tenants who don't take care of their living space. The best way to find out is by talking to them during escrow, and deciding if you'd like to keep them or cancel their lease once it's over.

It can be very costly to take on a mortgage loan; it's raised considerably from just a few years ago. Non-owner occupant properties have high fees, even the smaller loans under $100,000. But adding everything up, including the fees, title insurance, cost of escrow, appraisal costs, etc., can be anywhere up to 5 percent. Presently, rates are pretty competitive, and it's possible to get non-owner occupant financing for under 5 percent, as long as it's a 30-year mortgage. You'd be able to lock in that low-interest rate for those 30 years, which is definitely a positive.

So where exactly do you find these loans? The best option is to meet with a few different lenders and see which loans work best for what you'd want. You can look into it in either a couple different banks, a mortgage lender, and even online lenders. Each one will have different programs and different restrictions. If you get rejected by a bank, keep trying with others. A mortgage lender might accept you when the bank won't, so don't give up. Not only that, but the loans costs and interest rates vary depending on where you go, so make sure to compare across the board.

And what about the number of properties you can afford? Credit score is key here, so if you have a good one, plus good debt-to-income ratio, then you can probably finance up to about 4 different properties. Your debt-to-income ratio changes with each property, so keep that in mind too. It's possible to try even more than 4 properties, but you won't have a large number of lenders willing to help you finance. They are definitely some out there, but you'll have to look a little harder. Over 10 loans are even more difficult, but it's possible. There are lenders that specifically work with those who want over 10 loans, and they're called portfolio lenders.

Chapter 9: What are the Risks Involved?

There are definitely advantages to investing in rental properties. You can earn a lot of passive income and make great profits, all while maintaining financial security for the future. And while owning rental properties can be relatively safe, there are risks involved. It's good to practice diligence and ensure that if any of the negatives happen, you'll know how to turn it around quickly, before losing any money.

Vacancy: Having a high amount of vacancies is probably one of the worst things to happen to a rental property owner. Tenants are how you make your money and income, so going without them means you go without money. You can even reach a negative cash flow, meaning you have to start paying out of pocket for expenses. That can add up, and you end up losing a ton of money that you won't be able to make back. The best way to avoid this from happening, or at least lessen the blow is by purchasing rental properties in good neighborhoods. Do the proper research about the different areas; figure out which neighborhoods are safest, and which ones yield the best amenities. It might end up being a little more expensive to buy a property in a better neighborhood, but tenants are more likely to rent where they feel safe and where they have a lot of different things to choose from. Keeping a savings specifically for vacancies would probably be the smart thing to do, just in case you end up having to pay the mortgage, insurance, and property taxes from your own money.

Bad Tenants: While dealing with vacancies can mean you might lose money, having bad tenants can be so much worse. There's a large risk when taking in unknown people, and it requires you to be pretty selective. You need to do background checks, get references from previous landlords, ask for proof of income, run a credit check, and make sure to take a security deposit. If you end up with the wrong tenant, it could cost you a lot more than having the room empty for a bit. Make sure you also listen to what your gut is telling you. A person could be great on paper; have the necessary paperwork, have a great credit, and great references. But if there's just something odd about them, and they're giving you a strange vibe, then there might be something off about them that would mean they're not a good tenant. Trust yourself!

Cash Flow: Triple check the expenses and how much everything will cost you; even put in the cost of random maintenance that might actually never happen. Underestimating the cost could mean the end of your business and you owing thousands. Having the right team to help can make sure you don't accidentally forget something, but ultimately, it's up to you to remember. And it's not just considering the upfront costs, but how much everything will cost you each month. If you end up losing money every month because of not realizing the cost, you'll eventually be out of business from paying out of pocket.

The Right Time to Buy: Just like in other markets, the real estate market also has a sort of supply and demand. There's a constant fluctuate, so if you're thinking of maybe selling your property down the road, you might end up not making a profit. Investing in rental properties can cost a lot of money, especially up front, so you want to make sure that your expected return in the future makes is actually worth making the investment in the first place. The best thing to do is see if it's a seller's or buyer's market, and keep up with the trends. You want to buy in a buyer's market and sell once it's circled back around to a seller's market.

Theft: There's always a risk of your property becoming burglarized, especially if you're in a lower income location. If the crime rate is on the higher side, then you'll end up with a high turnover of tenants. Plus, what you charge for rent will be much lower than what you could charge in a higher income location. If burglary does happen a lot in your location, you could end up paying a lot of money in legal procedures and fees.

Foreclosure: If you end up not making enough profit, and can't meet your mortgage payments, then there's the change of your property being foreclosed. That's definitely the last thing you want because not only can it hurt you being approved for any future real estate loans, but word might get around, and no one would want to rent from you. Knowing the numbers and making sure you'll get a profit can help minimize the chance, plus making sure you have an emergency savings to help you out if needed.

Maintenance: Especially at the beginning, before you hire someone, you'll probably be the person your tenants call when something goes wrong. There's a high level of work involved when running rental properties, and that included maintenance issues. What happens when a pipe bursts? You can't just let it sit and hope it fixes itself. And if it happens in the middle of the night, there's a high chance that you won't be able to get anyone out to fix it until the next morning. Knowing basic maintenance can be very helpful as a landlord, and help you to save spending more money on issues that end up becoming a lot worse. Or if you're not very handy, you can hire a property manager that does know how to fix those types of thing. Keep in mind too that eventually, properties start to show their age. They typically start having structural damage, and major things would need replacing. It's best to keep up with everything, because if you let it go, then it'll just get worse and cost you a lot more money than necessary.

Airbnb: There's actually some risk to renting out property specifically for short-term rent, like Airbnb. You can make a lot of money doing it, but sometimes the local authorities put forth certain laws and restrictions for these types of businesses. You have to make sure that you pay all the different fees and taxes, and learn all the different local state and city laws about short-term rentals. Make sure to keep up with it because some laws might change and you could get into trouble if you don't change with them.

Chapter 10: How to Manage Your Properties

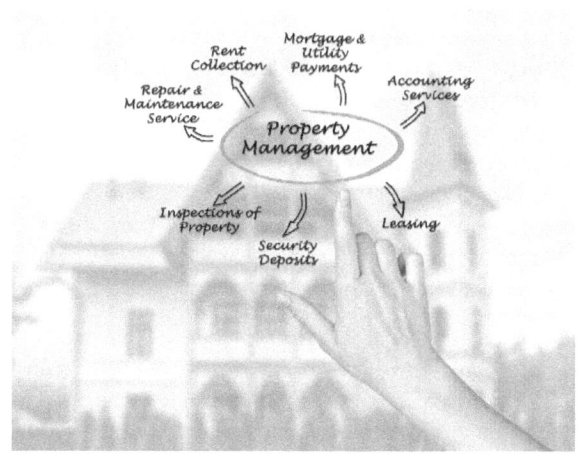

You basically have two options when it comes to managing your rental properties. You can either do it all yourself or hire a management company. Both have pros and cons, and it's really up to you with what works best for your style and business. A lot of the work and issues are at the beginning of the process when you're actually buying the property, which is good news. Basically, there's less work involved after getting the property, keep in mind that it still does take work. There's a specific process that goes into managing a rental, and each thing is handled differently depending on whether it's you or a management company.

Pre-Rent Repairs: It's always best to go around the property and determine what needs to be fixed before you even rent your property out. This is probably something that just you will be dealing with because typically property managers help with maintenance only after the property is rented. Knowing what kind of repairs the property needs and how much it's all going to cost is good to know even before buying the property, but you'll be able to get a better idea of how much work it will take once you do the walkthrough.

How Much is Rent: Knowing how much to rent the property for is determined by location, how much the house is worth, and how much you need in income. But what number you come up with might be different than the number a management company comes up with. A property manager wants to rent the property as quickly as possible because they collect their money based off of the rent. However, doing this might mean the property manager rents it for less than what it's worth, and you'll end up not making as much as you need.

Renting: Renting out the property can be a difficult process and frankly a little tedious. You need to find tenants, ones that you know will be good and make you the most money possible. That involves putting out advertisements for the property, showing your home, checking their credit, running a background check, creating a contract and lease, and collecting their money. You might start feeling frustrated and end up picking the tenant because they're the first to show up or they're the only ones willing to pay your asking price. You just have to remember to think in long run terms and remember that having patience when finding the right tenant will be worth it. Of course, this is where have a property manager comes in handy. You can let them know your specifications, and then leave everything in their hands. They can take care of the nitty gritty while you sit back and relax!

Money: It's very important that your tenants pay on time. You have mortgage payments to keep up with, and if they're late then your late. That reflects much worse on you then it does on them, so it's up to you to enforce timely payments. The best way to do this is by having late fees. And late fees are something you need to keep up with and be strict about. If you let one person slide, then everyone else will think it's ok. You might hear sob story after sob story, but you need to be firm and hold your ground. You might even have to start the eviction process if the tenant is very late, which could be the wake-up call they need. If you're the type of person that is very compassionate or kind-hearted, then it would probably be best to utilize a property manager for this process. They can be your go-between and collect the rent for you. It's their job to make sure the rent is collected on time and in full, so they would be perfectly fine with a harsher attitude and implementing the late fees.

Eviction: It's definitely a horrible process, and there are bad feelings all around when you have to evict a tenant. It's not something you like doing, and you risk the possibility of the tenant turning on you when you evict them. They might even take it out on you by trashing your property, which is the last thing you'd want to deal with. It's best to try to get a tenant to move out on good terms, so you don't have to worry about the room being messed up or dealing with what's owed. Just like collecting rent, if you'd rather not deal with the annoyance and hassle of evicting someone, a property management company can be a big help. You can leave the evictions up to them and not have to deal with upset or angry tenants. This is especially nice if you're worried about your safety; having another person with you when you're evicting someone is just good common sense.

Keep up with your houses: Even though you have a tenant, it's a good idea to do a walk through every once in a while. Your tenant might say they're keeping up with the house, but you really don't know unless you actually go over and look. The best way to do this without your tenant getting upset from you "invading" is by writing it in the lease. You can put in there that you have the right to do a property inspection at any time, as long as there's notice given. Most of the time, the notice is either 24 to 48 hours. That gives the tenant enough time to clean up anything they'd want to but not enough to hide any major issues. You can utilize this time to ensure that the property is being maintained well, check the smoke detectors and change the batteries if needed, and check to see if there are any other repairs needed. Many times, the biggest issues that happen are due to landlords who actually never check on their rental property. The tenant is paying on time every month and never seems to cause any problems, so that means the house is fine, right? Not exactly! The tenant could be on their best behavior because they're actually not keeping up with the house and destroying it. The worst kind of damage happens over a long period of time; a constant drip, an animal soiling the carpet, etc. Or maybe the tenant is doing something illegal and doesn't want you checking on the property for fear of being found out. If you really want to know what's going on in your house, then you should keep checking on it periodically yourself. You can hire a property manager, but they could just tell you they went to check on the house and never actually did it. You can never be completely sure unless you do it yourself. If you'd prefer a property manager though, then that's perfectly fine, but make sure to do a walk through at least once a month just to double check.

Maintenance: This isn't just something that happens during the pre-renting phase. As long as you have a property, then you'll need to do maintenance on it. Things will always break or need replacing, and it can be a lot of work to keep up with. You don't want properties that are broken down and obviously need a lot of work; tenants don't want to live in a place that has broken windows. To keep up with the maintenance issues, you should plan ahead for them by accounting them into your expense plan. That way, if something does happen then, it's completely fine because you've already planned for it. That's especially pertinent when there's water or electrical issues. You don't want your basement flooding because you couldn't afford to replace the pipes. These issues can happen at any time, and anywhere on your property, so you need to be prepared for that. Being prepared includes taking calls at 3 in the morning because of that pipe bursting. But if you prefer your sleep, that's where a property manager comes in handy. Instead of going to you about maintenance issues, the tenant can just call your property manager, and they can handle it. Obviously, they'll contact you if any work needs to be done, but it's nice to have a go-between taking care of the more difficult issues.

Legalese: It's important to keep track of all your expenses, rent amounts, profits, losses, etc. And if you're great at that sort of thing, then feel free to take it on! But having a property manager handle it all instead of you is pretty nice and means you don't have to worry about keeping track of everything. They can compile it all, and send it off to your accountant for review. You let them handle the dirty work and reap the benefits.

If you do decide to go with a property manager, remember to put that expense in your start-up costs. They can cut into what your profit will be, but keep in mind everything they'll do for you in return. They typically take around 8 to 12 percent of whatever the monthly rents add up to be, which really isn't that bad. Of course, when you're first starting out, usually it's with only one or two properties. Unless you're just extremely busy and have a lot of other stuff going on, then you probably don't need a property manager. But as you acquire more and more rental properties, then it would definitely make sense to hire some help. Think about it like this - if you are only renting out one property, then usually it takes only about a few hours every month to manage it, besides the process of finding tenants. You'll have to deal with collecting your rent, maintenance issues, and other small things, all which don't really add up too much time away from your day to day life. Even adding on another property or two still doesn't really take up that much time. However, once you've reached 4 or more rental properties, then that's when you begin to become overwhelmed. You might end up skimping out on the screening process for tenants or decide to slack on checking on your properties in person, both of which can cause you to lose some serious money. If you find yourself becoming overwhelmed and overworked, then get help in the form of a property manager. It's definitely worth that small fee for peace of mind and freedom of time.

Chapter 11: How to Know When to Exit

There might come a time when you're ready to sell your rental property. It makes sense to keep it long term, and there are many benefits to actually never selling. But maybe you're tired of dealing with tenants and repair issues, maybe it's a good time to sell, and you'd like to make a nice profit. Or maybe you just want to get out of the game. Regardless of your reasoning, there are some very specific factors to take into consideration when you realize it's time to sell your rental property:

Life: It happens, we get it. You can have a major life event, something that makes you reconsider owning your properties. Maybe a family member died, maybe you were laid off and no longer have the right funds to help support yourself, maybe you have to move across the country. You end up spending a lot of time and money focusing on whatever event is happening, so much so that you just don't have time to deal with your properties. It's possible that you can sell all of them, or maybe just downsize to one or two, enough for a little passive income.

More Money: It's entirely possible that you end up making a lot more money elsewhere. You could have another revenue source that really took off, or maybe you have a full-time job that just offered a great promotion. Rental income is considered passive income, but it also takes a lot of effort. If you can get more money from somewhere else that takes less effort, then it makes a lot more sense to go with that other option.

Not Enough Money: While you'd love if everyone loves your property, you have amazing tenants and are making a great income each month, there's a chance that you could end up with a negative cash flow instead. When investing in rentals, it's important to be making an income off of them in the first month. If you've gone months without any profits, and in fact are in the negatives, then maybe it's time to reevaluate this property and whether it's worth it.

Unhappy: Maybe you're just unhappy with how things are in your life now. You were excited about investing in rental properties at first, but now it's just too much work with no reward. Why would you keep doing something that makes you unhappy? Being a landlord can be a stressful job. That stress might be something you overlook because you're making great money and getting amazing profits. But eventually, it can become a burden and weigh pretty heavy on you. You end up with a ton of anxiety and stress that never really goes away. And not only is that a lot to deal with, but it's also extremely bad for your health! You don't want a heart attack just because you're unhappy in your job, do you?

Too Much: Real estate is all about supply and demand. If there are too many houses on the market, then the selling price will go down. That's definitely something you'd like to avoid, but it might be inevitable. While houses are sold and bought all the time, if there are new homes being built then it will be a very long time before it's a seller's market. Housing for sale or rent will become oversaturated and flooded. If you notice that there are a ton of new houses or condos being built, it's best to sell before they're finished, or you'll end up having to wait until it comes back around. Which could take decades, so you need to figure out if you want to keep renting that long or not.

Taxes: Property taxes are a pain. They can cause a lot of hassle and upset feelings, and they're something the local and state governments keep increasing instead of going somewhere else. Basically, if the local government has a big project in the works, like filling in all the potholes, they just decide to raise property taxes instead of increasing road tolls. This means that with higher property taxes, then the rent increases as well. The issue with this though is that increasing rent takes some time. It might say on your lease that you can't raise rent until the lease is over. And if that's not for another 8 months, then that's 8 months that you'll have to pay property taxes out of your own pocket. If you start seeing this trend happen a lot in your current city, it might make more sense to move to a state that is tax friendly. Fun fact, but Hawaii is actually the best state for dealing with property tax. It's ranked #50 at 0.28 percent, which means you'll be paying the lowest possible property tax out of all the states. Renting out a property as an Airbnb on Hawaii would probably be a great idea!

Commercial Real Estate: A great way to figure out whether or not residential housing is growing is by looking at how the commercial real estate scene is. Companies need to find a workspace before hiring people, so houses typically come second when there's about to be a big boom. You can look at this information and learn if there's a real estate slowdown happening. If companies aren't buying space in your area, then people probably aren't looking to move there any time soon.

Major Repairs: There are typical large expenses that happen like clockwork - a roof needs to be replaced every 10 to 20 years, a new water heater every 10 to 15 years, etc. These are normal, and you'll figure them into your housing costs at the beginning of the buying process. However, it's possible your property ends up needing repairs that cost more than it's worth. A law was recently passed in San Francisco that meant any housing units over a garage had to be retrofitted, which costs anywhere from $100,000 to $300,000. That's a lot of money to spend all at once, or even in a payment plan. You need to assess your property and decide if it's worth fixing or worth more just to sell it.

Natural Disasters: Does your area have any natural disasters? Specific areas can be more susceptible to things like flooding, fires, hurricanes, etc. It's best to research your area and figure out which natural disaster is the norm and how often it hits. Hurricanes hit the Gulf coast every year, but the really deadly ones only hit every 5 to 10 years. If you know, it's been a few years since a disaster has struck, or if you have decided to opt out of the natural disaster insurance, then maybe it's a good idea to sell. You could end up losing your house and be left with the land, in which it would be very expensive to try and rebuild.

Commission Rates: The commission rate for real estate agents has been steady at a very high 5 percent, which isn't much of a difference from the 6 percent that was ten years ago! The main issue is that half of the 5 percent, 2.5 percent, goes to the buyer's real estate agent. They obviously want the best possible deal for their client, which means the best possible deal for them. You're basically paying the buyer's real estate agent instead of their own client. And most real estate agents try to find listings that have the 2.5 percent commission, so if yours doesn't, then it will be doubly difficult to sell. If by some chance the commission rate goes down, then take the chance before it changes again by selling.

Appreciate the Property: There is such a thing as the property having "appreciation." This is when the value of the property goes up, and it becomes worth it to sell. Let's say you decide to invest in a fixer-upper for your rental property. You completely overhaul it; new furniture, new appliances, new everything. Your plan is to rent it out, and you're successfully making a great profit from it. However, there's a chance that because the property is so great now, and if the location becomes more up and coming and hip, then the value of the property goes way up. When that happens, you need to decide whether you'd like to keep renting it out or sell it. If you do sell, you could use some of that money to put back into a different property instead.

Conclusion

Thank you for making it through to the end of *Rental Property Investing: How to Create Wealth and Passive Income Through Intelligent Real Estate Investing*. Let's hope it was informative and able to provide you with all of the tools you need to achieve your goals whatever they may be.

The next step is to figure out where you go from here. It might be best to start slow, maybe even speak to several real estate investors for their opinions and how they got started. Or you could just jump right in and start researching properties and their locations. Remember, location is everything to your success, so it's best to look up several properties and then look around at the different amenities they have. You could even do it opposite; if there's an area that you really like and know will do really well, look up if there are any properties for sale in it. Look at apartments, single family homes, and multi-family homes to see which ones you'd prefer and which ones would do the best in the area you're interested in. And don't forget, you can look at the properties first, but make sure your direct next step is figuring out exactly how much you can afford. You'll need to know the exact number you're fine with spending in closing costs so that you know what to do when negotiating. There's a lot of work that goes into real estate investing, especially when it's rentals. But this book can really help you figure things out without getting overwhelmed and truly help you to succeed.

Finally, if you found this book useful in any way, a review on Amazon is always appreciated!

Day Trading:

Make Money With These Simple Strategies, the Ultimate Guide to Mastering the Art of Trading

Table of Contents

Introduction

Chapter 1: Day Trading Basics

Chapter 2: Starting Off Strong

Chapter 3: Trading Strategies to Know

Chapter 4: Momentum Trading

Chapter 5: Tips for Success

Conclusion

Copyright 2018 by Gilles Flebus - All rights reserved.

The follow eBook is reproduced below with the goal of providing information that is as accurate and reliable as possible. Regardless, purchasing this eBook can be seen as consent to the fact that both the publisher and the author of this book are in no way experts on the topics discussed within and that any recommendations or suggestions that are made herein are for entertainment purposes only. Professionals should be consulted as needed prior to undertaking any of the action endorsed herein.

This declaration is deemed fair and valid by both the American Bar Association and the Committee of Publishers Association and is legally binding throughout the United States.

Furthermore, the transmission, duplication or reproduction of any of the following work including specific information will be considered an illegal act irrespective of if it is done electronically or in print. This extends to creating a secondary or tertiary copy of the work or a recorded copy and is only allowed with express written consent from the Publisher. All additional right reserved.

The information in the following pages is broadly considered to be a truthful and accurate account of facts and as such any inattention, use or misuse of the information in question by the reader will render any resulting actions solely under their purview. There are no scenarios in which the publisher or the original author of this work can be in any fashion deemed liable for any hardship or damages that may befall them after undertaking information described herein.

Additionally, the information in the following pages is intended only for informational purposes and should thus be thought of as universal. As befitting its nature, it is presented without assurance regarding its prolonged validity or interim quality. Trademarks that are mentioned are done without written consent and can in no way be considered an endorsement from the trademark holder.

Introduction

Congratulations on downloading Day Trading: Make Money With These Simple Strategies, the Ultimate Guide to Mastering the Art of Trading and thank you for doing so. If you already have some experiencing trading in one of the securities markets and are looking for something a little more hands on that has extreme profit potential, then day trading is what you have been waiting for.

Regardless of your level of overall trading experience, transitioning to day trading isn't a one-to-one affair which is why the following chapters will discuss everything you need to know in order to get started day trading successfully. First, you will learn what sets day trading apart from more traditional types of trading as well as what to expect when you get your feet wet. Next, you will learn how to get started day trading on the right foot in order to minimize the transition period as much as possible.

From there, you will learn a variety of useful trading strategies including pairs trading, contrarian trading, fading, midday trading and more. You will then find a deep dive into the many benefits of momentum trading while day trading and how you can best put this strategy to work for you. Finally, you will find a number of tips for success and mistakes to avoid to ensure you are able to find success in your new trading venture as quickly as possible.

There are plenty of books on this subject on the market, thanks again for choosing this one! Every effort was made to ensure it is full of as much useful information as possible, please enjoy!

Chapter 1: Day Trading Basics

Broadly speaking, day trading is similar to any other type of securities trading except that positions are often held for far less time and the overall trades tend to be larger. Most trades of this type are rarely held for more than a few minutes at a time, and they are practically never held overnight. As such, the first thing you are going to need in order to ensure your time spent day trading is as fruitful as possible is an intimate understanding of the market in which you plan to day trade.

While there will obviously be some differences when day trading in different markets, there are always going to be a number of steps that are the same. First, you will need to locate an underling asset that you are interested in trading based on your research which should be based on either fundamental or technical analysis. Second, you will need to decide if it aligns with your personal trading plan as just because a trade is potential profitable doesn't mean it is going to be the right choice for you, right now. From there, assuming you are still interested in making the trade, you can then take a position that you believe will soon be profitable based on the current state of the market. Finally, you will do the same thing around 100 times a day.

Pros and cons of day trading

While the above description might make it sound as though day trade is relatively straightforward, the fact of the matter is that it is an extremely complex process requiring the successful use of a variety of tools and skills that not everyone will be able to follow through on reliably. As such, this list of pros and cons should make it easier for you to determine if this type of trading is one that you are interested pursuing in the long-term in search of your ultimate financial goals.

Pros: The biggest pro when it comes to day trading is the potential for gain when everything goes according to plan. The average successful day trader tends to buy a large number of shares at a time to ensure that they stand to make a serious profit from even an extremely small amount of movement. Additionally, they have the potential to work for themselves, only trading when they feel the urge or when the market is in a place that is too good to pass up.

Another major benefit to day trading for certain types of traders is the amount of excitement they can expect to see on a daily basis. As they only ever trade in the absolute shortest timeframes, the average day trader sees far more action than most other types of traders would in the same amount of time. What's more, day trading provides those who are up to the challenge with the opportunity to face off with many of the best traders in the world, dozens, if not hundreds of times each day. If you are the sort of thrill seeker who is sure to appreciate a good spike of adrenaline then day trading might be for you.

Another benefit to day trading is that you can teach yourself as easily as you can pay someone else to teach you what to do, making it one of the few ways you can get a job in the financial sector with a formal education. As long as you are willing and able to put in the time and dedicated enough to see it through to the end, then there is no reason you can't acquire the skills you need on your own and then hone them through countless hours of practice.

Cons: The biggest downside to day trading has to do with the wide variety of costs associated with being able to do so successfully. As they are dealing with very small amounts of movement, day traders need a sizeable amount of trading capital just to get off the ground. An amount of around $20,000 should be enough to let you get started in a truly productive fashion. Beyond that, the number of daily trades being made means that the costs paid in commission are going to be far higher than with most other types of trading.

Not only that but due to the high number of shares that come along with the average trade in this field, the potential for loss if a trade turns against you can be quite significant as well. In fact, statistically speaking, day trading is the most difficult type of securities trading to make a profit from in any sort of reliable fashion. In fact, a majority of new day traders experience mostly losses for at least the first month, and only about 30 percent move on from that state to be able to reliably turn a profit.

What's more, the monetary issues aren't the only barriers to entry either, and one of the biggest is the fact that the average amateur day trader is generally competing against professional organizations with a cadre of traders at their disposal and pockets that are extremely deep. As such, if you want to hope to chance of entering the market successfully then you will need to be prepared for what you are up against. Finally, many brokerages will simply not let you day trade in any way shape or form until you have already proven that you are capable of trading in a competent fashion on a more manageable scale to start.

In addition to these issues, the fact that the average day trader is self-employed means that it will simply not be the right choice for those who don't have the internal fortitude to put in the required work without having a boss standing over your shoulder ensuring that they are doing all that is needed for them to be successful. What's more, the average day trader has to fend for themselves when it comes to things like health insurance, a steady retirement plan or even a steady paycheck.

Key terms

Long: A long position is taken by a trader when they purchase a given stock, currency pair or option.

Short: A short position is taken by a trader when they sell a given stock, currency pair or option.

Bear market: A market that is trending towards lower prices across the board is said to be a bear market.

Bull market: A market that is trending towards high prices across the board is said to be a bull market.

Bid price: The bid price of a given stock is the price that traders are currently willing to pay for it. This does not need to be the same as the ask price.

Ask price: The ask price of a given stock is the price that sellers are currently selling the stock for. It does not need to match up with the bid price.

Spread: The spread is the difference between the bid price and the ask price.

Open: The open price is what a given stock is worth at the start of the trading day.

Close: The close price is what a given stock is worth at the end of the trading day.

Slippage: Slippage is the difference between the price of a specific ask or bid between when you go to make a trade and when that trade goes through.

Intraday range: The intraday range is the difference between the low point and the high point of a stock's price over a predetermined number of days.

Volume: Volume is the number of shares of a given stock that trade hands during the trading day.

Liquidity: Liquidity refers to how difficult a given stock is to obtain. Widely available stocks have high liquidity and stocks that are hard to find have low liquidity. As a general rule, the more liquidity a given stock has, the lower its price is going to be.

Volatility: Volatility refers to the amount which a specific stock is going to change over time. The more volatility a stock has, the more it is likely to change.

Knowing what leads to follow

Premarket movers: If the market hasn't opened yet, then the price of a given stock is always going to be subject to change. Nevertheless, it is still going to be an excellent place to start when it comes to deciding if a given stock is going to be worth trading on a certain day. The first thing you will need to be on the lookout for is those with a greater than average amount of volatility for the previous 30 days before checking to determine if the price at close lower or higher than average as well.

Social media: These days, there are just as many social media groups dedicated to the ins and outs of the markets as there are more official sources, and many of them manage to get the early scoop on the comings and goings of the market quite frequently. This, in turn, will make it easier for you to determine how the market is likely going to move before it has a chance to get started which will make it easier for you to get in on the ground floor of beneficial changes.

Earnings Calendar: A surefire way to see an increase in volatility is when earnings are reported. You are never going to want to jump on an assumed trend before they are released but shortly thereafter the trade gates will be thrown wide open.

Chapter 2: Starting Off Strong

When it comes to getting started with day trading successfully, there are a number of obstacles that are going to be standing in your way. Luckily, once you know what to be on the lookout for, things should proceed far more smoothly, which is why this chapter will outline the key things you need to do in order to start off on the right foot when it comes to day trading.

Find the right broker

Look closely at your current broker: Due to the fact that day trading should never be your first type of trading, it is likely that you already have a broker of some type. As such, in order to ensure you are on the right track, the first thing you will need to do is to ensure that this broker is still going to be the right choice now that your needs are changing dramatically. If you decide to wait until you already feel as though you are missing out on profits then it is too late and the damage has been done. Getting this out of the way early will help ensure that your day trading career is as profitable as possible right from the start.

Think about unique requirements: In order to ensure you find the best broker possible, the first thing you will want to do is consider the requirements that are an absolute dealer breaker when it comes to functionality. While you may well not have any special requirements, if you do and you don't put them first then you are sure to end up being disappointed in the long run.

Consider the fees: As a day trader, you are going to be making far more trades than you previously were in most cases which means that the type and amount of fees that you are paying are going to become far more important that in previously was. While you will know to look at the cost of commissions, it is also important to be on the lookout for fees regarding things like data, platform, withdrawals and even inactivity.

Other limitations: Additionally, many brokers commonly place additional limitations that individuals must meet if they plan on day trading, including significantly increased minimum balance amounts as well as proven general trading competency to ensure they aren't appearing to take advantage of those who are clearly ill-informed. You will also need to consider the type of margin you are going to be dealing with and the differences between trading in the forex or stock market. Finally, it is important to consider any promotions the brokerage might be running at the moment as you never know what kind of deals you may get.

Research, research, research: After you have narrowed down your search somewhat, the next thing you are going to need to do is to look more closely at each of the companies you are now seriously considering to ensure they are completely on the level and to ensure you aren't giving your hard earned trading capital to a fly-by-night organization. Assuming your broker is located in the United States (and if you are then it should be as well) then you will be able to consult either the National Future Association for details about forex and futures brokers or the Financial Industry Regulatory Authority for details of various stock brokers. Both of these organizations should be able to provide you with a great deal of insight into the broker in question, including if any type of punitive action has been taken against them.

Beyond the report from the organization in question, it is also extremely important to look at user reviews, after all, they are the ones who will actually be in the best situation to know what's what. While a few bad reviews here and there are nothing to worry about, if it looks as though there are negative trends forming over many reviews then you may want to reconsider your choice.

Brokers based in the United States are often regulated by a voluntary regulatory body that, theoretically, keeps them in check and ensures they treat their customers properly. Even if you aren't based in the US then you are still going to want to choose a local broker if possible as otherwise, you have very few guarantees that anyone will even try to help you should they disappear with your money. While brokers abroad likely have better deals, the potential for additional risk is such that it is rarely going to balance out the additional risk.

Get in touch: Once you have narrowed down your list, even more, the next thing you are going to do is consider the quality of their customer service. To do so, the first thing you will want to do is look on their website for a phone number to call, not an email address but an actual phone number. While you likely won't need to communicate with your broker in person much at all, when you do the odds are high that it will be an emergency which means you need to know beforehand if you are likely to get a response. As such, if they don't have a phone number where you can reach them then you are going to want to move on.

Once you do give a number a call, the next step is to see how long it takes them to get back to you, assuming you don't connect with someone directly. If you are forced to leave a message then take note of the time as if they don't get back to you within one business day then you are going to want to take your business elsewhere. After all, if they can't be bothered to return the call of a potential client in a reasonable time, the odds that they will treat you any better once they already have your money is extremely thin. After you do successfully get a hold of someone you will want to call back again once or twice with a trumped up issue, just to see how they go about handling it, just to ensure they live up to their first impressions.

Start small: Once you find a new broker that seems as though it is going to work for you, the last step is going to be actually funding the account up to the minimum allowable amount and then making a few trades to ensure that everything works out as advertised. After you make a number of trades successfully then you can begin to increase your confidence in your new broker and your account with them along with it. You will still want to be on the lookout for things like unexpected fees or service outages, but after a few months without complaints you can likely let your guard down safely.

Tools of the trade

Computer: While your existing laptop or aging PC likely served your basic trading needs with aplomb, the difference between success and failure when day trading can come down to a matter of a few seconds. Thus, it stands to reason that if you are working with outdated technology you run the risk of being at a serious disadvantage when compared to your properly kitted out competition. While this doesn't mean you need the best of the best, though a good computer never hurt anyone, it does mean that the rig you are using needs to be able to run all the latest and greatest software without a hitch.

To this end, you will need to ensure that your CPU is up to date and that you have the extra ram to spare when it comes to being able to run multiple live data feeds all at once along with various charts and other information that is relevant at the moment. You are also going to want to ditch the laptop for something with a little more stopping power, and a far greater degree of customization potential.

The first reason that this is the case is that you are either going to need one very nice graphics card or two average graphics cards to ensure that you can run a minimum of two monitors, though three is really ideal. Three monitors positioned in a vertical fashion will allow you to see the most accurate information as possible, constantly being updated in real time which is just what you are going to need in order to ensure you never miss a potential opening. While such a setup might seem excessive at first, the fact of the matter is that there are serious benefits to being able to have a display that is dedicated to a trading platform, another that is dedicated to the news and still another that is dedicated solely to analytical information.

A robust internet connection: Much like with your computer, while you can possibly get by with the level of online service you currently have, in order to ensure that you can confidently trade without issue you are going to need to be ready to pony up for a more serious online pipeline. Specifically, this means knowing your current amount of bandwidth in combination with the amount of latency that you are going to be dealing with as well as the ways in which you can make all the various numbers as low as possible.

To ensure your latency is as manageable as possible you are going to want to find a broker that is as close to your physical location as possible as the closer you are to the source the faster your trade orders will be processed. Furthermore, you are going to want to pay an extra $20 a month to ensure you have DSL access as well. While this might seem excessive, the first time you don't miss out on a trade thanks to your phoneline the entire backup will likely pay for itself and then some.

Useful data: The simple fact of the matter is that you can't ever hope to be a successful trader if you don't have the right data to consider prior to making any trades. While a lot of what you are going to be tracking is going to vary based on the strategies you are using and the markets you favor, you will always want to keep an eye on the news to ensure you don't miss out on any major trends that are building in the future. While there is any number of options that require you to pay for the news, you can likely find most of the same information for free by paying attention to the Twitter feeds of the big names in the markets you favor.

Another extremely useful piece of economic data is the Bloomberg Economic Calendar. This calendar contains a list of all of the various dates and deadlines that the movers and shakers in the market are currently dealing with. As a day trader, it is important that you are aware of all of these days as letting them pass you by is akin to trading blind which is really just asking for trouble. It is also important to use a website or software that works to narrow down potential trades worth investigating more closely to ensure you can do more with your time that separate good potential trades from the bad.

Comfort items: It is important to keep in mind that, as a day trader, you are going to be spending a large portion of each day staring at a bunch of computer screens for hours on end which means you need to think about the physical concerns that come along with doing so. It is important that you think about your body in addition to your bank account if you hope to make things work in the long-term.

One great place to start is by replacing your normal desk with one of the standing variety. Studies show that standing while you work will not only serve to make you more focused on the task you are currently working on, it will actually help burn calories and prevent numerous different negative side effects associated with too much sitting from taking hold. You can easily find a simple addition to your standard desk to change the height for around $100 or you can find something more complicated that raises the entire desk space for $700 or more, the route you take doesn't matter, as long as you start standing.

Even if you are standing for a majority of your day, you still have to sit sometime and when you do it is important you put an equal amount of thought into your chair as well as your desk. While choosing something that is designed with ergonomics in mind might cost more up front, the benefits to your posture and back are too numerous to list.

Next on the list is some type of entertainment, because you are going to be spending long stretches of time staring at a screen with numbers that just don't want to cooperate. It is vital that you do something to keep your mind sharp so that you don't miss the ideal entry point when it does present itself because your brain had already switched to autopilot. Just be sure to choose something that doesn't require all of your attention, you do still need to be working after all.

Chapter 3: Trading Strategies to Know

Trade the news: When it comes to trading the news successfully, you will want to use major news events as a means of predicting the direction the market is likely to move once it catches wind of the news. It is vital that you keep up with news from around the world, as you never know when something unexpected is going to happen that affects the market in a significant way. While you may never be able to hear about every incoming news story reliably, if you do keep your ear to the ground and hear something juicy, you would then be able to take advantage of their understanding of the market and buy or sell accordingly to ensure they make the most profit.

If you plan on using this strategy on a regular basis then you need to understand that the early news bird catches the trend worm which means that if you don't hop on these sorts of trends first thing in the morning then you may as well move on to another strategy as the potential to profit from this one will have long since expired for the day. Get ahead of the game and learn about the news and make your trades early in the day so you can still get the best prices, either in buying or selling, before anyone else does.

To be clear, trading the news entails doing research on prevailing trends in the markets you favor to ensure that you have a fairly good idea of what the news is going to be when you hear about it along with everyone else so that you can get to work while other traders are still floundering. This is different than insider trading, which involves taking advantage of proprietary information to stack the deck in your favor. For example, if you hold stocks in a trade and hear from a friend that this company is going to declare bankruptcy the following day, you may decide that now is a good time to sell your stocks. But when you do this before the company announces their bankruptcy, you could be participating in illegal activity.

Pivot points: In order to take advantage of this strategy it is important that you first become extremely familiar with the specific securities that you prefer to work with day in and day out so that you have a general understanding of their high and low points, thus making it easier to predict where it is likely they are going to go next.

If you don't have access to this type of first-hand information then you can use existing historical charts to make do, as long as you can clearly determine the highs and lows for the security in question. In order to ensure this strategy works as well as possible, you will need to have a clear top and bottom determined. You will then simply buy or sell based on not where the security is currently going, but where it is likely to go once it rounds the pivot point and starts back the other way.

Essentially, you are going to look at these charts and try to figure out where the lowest and the highest points are. When the stock gets to the lowest point, it is time to enter the market and purchase the stock at a lower price, hopefully, lower than market value. You will then hold onto the stock for a bit, waiting for it to reach the high point on the chart, or at least higher than where you started so that you can make a profit when it's time to sell.

Pairs trading: As the name implies, pairs trading is a strategy wherein you choose a general category of stocks, tech stocks for example, and then go short on one stock in the sector while going long on the other. Making these trades at the same time will bolster your odds of ensuring one of them actually turns a profit while also ensuring that you are able to turn a profit regardless of the conditions in the market. You will also be able to see movement on all sides more easily including sideways movement, downtrends, and uptrends and then bet on a few different options within the market. Since you are betting on both sides, you are more likely to make some money compared to just picking one kind of stock.

Contrarian trading: This is a strategy that you should like hold off on pursuing until you have had a bit of experience when it comes to day trading. Essentially, this strategy boils down to making trades that are the opposite of what the current trend would imply makes sense, so that when things do turn around you are in an extremely strong position. When using this type of trading you will need to pick out an asset that is currently underperforming which will ensure that you can buy in for essentially a song and a prayer. You will then simply hold the stock in question until it goes up. Even if the positive growth is only marginal, the price you purchased it for should ensure that you are still able to turn a substantial profit.

Contrarian traders often believe that when people say that the market is heading up, they are saying this because they have invested themselves too much and don't have the purchasing power that they once had and so the market it now at its peak. But on the other side, when people in the market are predicting a downturn, they have already sold their securities, meaning that the market now has room to go up.

Useful contrarian indicators to keep in mind include those that do their best to emphasize securities that are already out of favor. However, this does not mean that you are only going to pick stocks exclusively because they are out of favor, as most stocks are often priced as they are for a reason. Instead, you are going to want to keep an eye out for a stock whose fundamentals are improving and the market hasn't noticed yet, or those that are experiencing an unexpected upturn or downturn at the moment. These are all signs that the market is currently operating incorrectly which means you will need to buy in soon because the market is sure to correct its mistakes sooner than later.

Fading: The fading strategy involves shorting a stock as soon as it finishes a period of rapid growth. To know you have found the right stock, the first thing you are going to want to do is to ensure that the stock is overbought, which you can tell by noting when the buyers who got in early start to take their profits. This, in turn, will cause new buyers to think twice about the market turning around. This will ultimately quite, however, as the buyers are likely to step back in once or twice more before the bottom falls out of the stock in question. As such, purchasing during the initial slump will give you a clear sign of where things are going and when you will want to jump back out.

Using this strategy you can buy into stocks that are high-priced overall, for a lower-than-average market value, while also not having to wait very long for the price to correct itself and likely even move somewhat higher. In order to use this strategy successfully, it is important that you learn enough about the market to read when the stock in question is overpriced, as well as accurately predict when early buyers are likely to start selling off their shares. While this strategy does inherently come with some extra risk, with practice you will be able to identify the window when you will be able to make your move.

Trade during the midday: While conventional wisdom says that the early hours of a trading are when all the real action happens, there is still plenty of action to take advantage of during the midday as long as you know where to look. The biggest benefit to trading during this time period is going to be the fact that the trends that are still moving are likely to be far more well-established than what you will see during the earlier parts of the day. This is when many professional traders do a lot of their business, which means it is important to be ready with your relevant research so you have a firm idea of what trends to follow.

Scalping

Basic scalping: If you are just getting started with day trading and don't want to put a lot of money on the line per trade, then scalping is a great place to start, though it does require lots of micromanaging, as well as fast reflexes, in order to work to its full potential. Scalping is all about making as many surefire trades as possible during the day which means getting out almost as soon as you see any profit whatsoever. While you will only make a few dollars per trade, if you can do it 100 times per day, several days each week you will be well on your way to being able to trade full time.

Scalping correctly means keeping a close eye on the bid-ask spread which is the difference between what buyers are willing to pay and what sellers are willing to sell for. If you hope to make a profit you need to find a security where the gap between the bid and the ask is wide enough for you to do some work in. When the spread is wider than normal it means there is a higher demand to buy than there is to sell so other traders are going to be selling at a point that is above the traditional asking price.

On the contrary, if the bid/ask spread is narrow, then this means that there is a greater than average demand to sell, while only minimal interest in buying. If you encounter this scenario then it is a good time to purchase the security in question as you will almost certainly be able to get it for a stellar price. You will then be able to hold onto the security for a bit until the bid ask price gets back to normal levels or even with the wider gap again.

An additional important point to keep in mind is that when scalping it is extremely important to pay attention to the commissions that you are paying as it is easy to spend so much on fees that your profits take a serious hit. Ideally, you will want to pay a commission that scales based on the overall cost of the trade you are making as opposed to a scenario where you pay a fixed rate per trade regardless of the amounts involved.

Scalping forex: If you decide to work with scalping in the forex markets, know that some of your major competitors are algorithms so expect that they can beat you to the ideal spreads. This does not mean that you won't be able to catch some profit, but that the ideal time to sell is almost never made since you simply won't be able to react as fast as a computer program. In many ways, scalpers are the original day traders, and you will never hold onto a commodity for longer than a few minutes, or hours at most. You will always want to cash out at the end of the day because you are trading without knowing anything about the underlying assets you purchase.

Capital and cycles: When scalping in the forex markets you are going to want to ensure that your spreads are less than three pips, which is three percent of the total cost of the currency in question. If you are trading in the stock market then you will want to ensure the spread is less than two dollars. For both, your capital requirements are going to differ. If you are trading in the stock market then you will want to focus on making anywhere between 10 and 30 trades each day, taking care to only ever invest about five percent of your total trading capital into any one stock. While you will be holding onto these stocks far longer than you would as a forex trader, though still less than four hours on average.

If you plan on scalping in the stock market, then you will work in roughly the same way that someone who focused mainly on trading the news would in that they don't care specifically if a trend is negative or positive, only that it is large enough to follow through on. As you will be looking at cycles as they appear throughout the day you can expect your average trading day to be much longer than if you were pursuing another form of trading. Specifically, you will want to block out 10 hour periods where you can focus on the market and only start trading when you hit the six hour mark or so, once you can say with confidence that you understand what trades are starting to form.

You will cash out several times in each stock and will be doing so based on your prediction of the cycle. The reason that this works is that news events fluctuate the price of a stock quite heavily but typically settle down as the end of the day starts to draw near, depending on the news that dropped that day, of course. However, throughout the day the stock will still likely bounce between support and resistance levels, which is where you will make your moves depending on the current nature of the swing. Remember, you should only be focused on buying when the spread is narrow and selling when it is wide.

A spread of three pips on a micro lot isn't going to be much, but the fluctuation you are looking for is going to be fractions of a dollar. Your investments here should be about 2-4% of your investment fund. You will want at least four hundred to eight hundred invested in any given currency pair. Generally speaking, you will rarely hold any of these positions for more than 30 minutes at a time. While there is no hard and fast science behind choosing the right time to ender, you will always want to make your decisions based on the spread while aiming to keep it low.

At the same time, your exit strategy will need to be a function of the amount of profit you need to make in order to feel as though you are not wasting your time. As such, the more invested you are in a specific currency pair, the less time you will have to hold it. It is important to invest as heavily in a given currency pair as possible when you do make a move as the more units of the currency you own the less movement you will need to risk in order to ensure you turn a profit. Generally speaking, you are far more likely to be successful starting off scalping in the stock market if you have limited funds and then working your way up to the level of capital that scalping in forex realistically requires.

In order to start scalping in the forex market successfully, you are going to want to have in hand a minimum of $20,000. Remember, like all trading capital this needs to be money that you have saved, not that you have borrowed and it also needs to be money that is not actively earmarked for anything more specific. If you cut corners when it comes to getting your forex scalping capital together you will end up focusing more on the money that you can't afford to lose than the optimal trades to make at the moment, causing your worst fears to come true more often than not. As such, the best choice is always not to rush, trade with what you can afford, save your profits and repeat.

Choosing stocks: Volatility is the key. You are looking for stocks are destined to have several jumps throughout the day, hoping to get on low and sell when high. The best determinates of this are any mention in the news of a company. This will not only affect the company in question but quite possibly the entire sector that the company is a part of. News about Facebook has an effect on Twitter. News about Dunkin Donuts has an effect on Starbucks and McDonalds. Ideally, you will want to look for companies with smaller spreads as well as those that are in the news, or whose competition that is in the news when it comes to locking in your daily picks.

Choosing currency pairs: Choosing currency pairs is far more about experience when it comes to scalping as there are many variables to keep in mind. Specifically, everything is going to revolve exclusively around the spread. The only hard and fast advice when it comes to scalping forex currencies is that exotic currencies work well as they are frequently underutilized. This includes pairs like USD/MXN and USD/KRR; these will be more volatile and have more swings throughout the day. Assuming you are coming in with an appropriate amount of capital, then you will be able to trade both major and minor currency pairs which will typically have narrower spreads, allowing you to place more trades as the day progresses.

Chapter 4: Momentum Trading

Momentum is at the heart of all day trading as finding trades with the right amount of momentum is the only way you can reliably guarantee a profit on your trades. Luckily, it is not unrealistic to expect to find at least one underlying asset that is likely to move as much as 30 percent each day due to the fact that all underlying assets with this much momentum all tend to share a few common technical indicators.

Momentum stock anatomy

While it might seem difficult to understand how anyone could expect to pick a stock with the right momentum out of the thousands of possible choices, the fact of the matter is that all high momentum stocks typically have several things in common. In fact, if you were given a list of 5,000 stocks, using the factors below you could likely come up with a list of 10 or less.

Float: The first thing you are going to want to keep in mind is that the stocks with the highest momentum are generally going to have a float that is less than 100 million shares. Float refers to the total number of shares that are currently available and can be found by taking the total number of outstanding shares and subtracting out all those that are restricted or are, functionally speaking, no longer traded. Restricted shares are those that are currently in the midst of a lockup period or other, similar restriction. The less float a stock has, the more volatility it is going to contain. Stocks with smaller float tend to have low liquidity and a higher bid/ask spread.

Daily charts: The next thing you are going to want to look for is stocks that are consistently beating their moving average and trending away from either the support or resistance depending on if you following a positive or negative trend.

Relative volume: You are also going to want to ensure that the stocks you are considering have a high amount of relative volume, with the minimum being twice what the current average is. The average you should consider in this case would be the current volume compared to the historical average for the stock in question. The standard volume is going to reset every night at midnight which means this is a great indicator when it comes to stocks that are seeing a higher than average amount of action right now.

Catalyst: While not, strictly speaking, required, you may still find it helpful to look for stocks that are currently having their momentum boosted by external sources. This can include things like activist investors, FDA announcements, PR campaigns and earnings reports.

Exit indicators to watch

Besides knowing what a potentially profitable momentum trade looks like, you are also going to need to know what to look for to ensure that you can successfully get while the getting is good. Keep the following in mind and you will always be able to get out without having to sacrifice any of your hard earned profits.

Don't get greedy: It is important to set profit targets before you go into any trade, and then follow through on them when the trade turns in your favor. If you find yourself riding a stronger trend than you initially anticipated, the best choice is to instead sell off half of your holdings before setting a new and improved price target for the rest, allowing you to have your cake and eat it too.

Red candles: If you are not quite at your price target and you come across a candle that closes in the red then this is a strong indicator that you should take what you have and exit ASAP. If you have already sold off half of your holdings at this point, however, then you are going to want to go ahead and hold through the first red candle as long as it doesn't go so far as to actively trigger your stop loss.

Extension bar: An extension bar is a candle with a spike that causes dramatically increased profits. If this occurs you want to lock in your profits as quickly as possible as it is unlikely to last very long. This is your lucky day and it is important to capitalize on it.

Choosing a screener

Another important aspect of using a momentum strategy correctly is using a quality stock screen in order to find stocks that are trending towards the extreme ends of the market based on the criteria outlined above. A good screener is a virtually indispensable tool when it comes to narrowing down the field of potential options on any given day, the best of the best even let you generate your own unique filters that display a list of stocks that meet a variety of different criteria. What follows is a list of some of the most popular screeners on the market today.

StockFetchter.com: StockFetcher.com is one of the more complicated screeners out there, but all that complexity comes with a degree of power that is difficult to beat. Its power comes from a virtually unlimited number of parameters that its users can add to filter, ensuring that you only see exactly the types of stocks you are looking for. It offers a free as well as a paid version, the free version allows you to see the top five stocks that match your parameters while the paid version, $8.95 per month, shows you unlimited results.

Finviz.com: This site offers a wide variety of different premade filters that are designed to return results on the most promising stocks for a given day. It is extremely user friendly as well and functions from three drop-down menus based on the type of indicator, technical, fundamental or descriptive, and lets you choose the criteria for each. The results can then be sorted in a myriad of different ways to make it as easy to find the types of stocks you are looking for as possible. The biggest downside to Finviz is that it uses delayed data which means it is going to be most effective for those who run evening screens so they are ready to go when the market opens.

Chartmill.com: This site allows users to filter stocks based on a number of predetermined criteria including things like price, performance, volume, technical indicators and candlestick patterns. It also offers up a number of more specialized indicators including things like squeeze plays, intensity, trend and pocket pivots. This site works based on a credit system, and every user is given 6,000 credits each month for free. Every scan costs a few hundred credits so you should be able to take advantage of a variety of their tools virtually free of charge. Additional credits then cost $10 per 10,000 or they have an unlimited option available for about $30 per month.

Stockrover.com: This tool is specifically designed to cater to the Canadian market in addition to the US stock market. It offers up a variety of fundamental filters in addition to technical and performance based options. This tool also allows you to track stocks that are near their established lows and high, those that may be gaining momentum and even those that are seeing a lot of love from various hedge funds. Users also have the ability to create custom screens as well as unique equations for even more advanced screening. Users can also backtest their ideas to make sure that everything is working as intended. While their basic options are free to use, the more complex choices are gated behind a paywall that costs $250 for a year's subscription.

Know your filters

Day trading is about more than finding stocks that are high in volume, it is also about finding those that are currently experiencing a higher than average degree of movement as well. The following filters will help ensure that the stocks you find have plenty of both.

Steady volatility: In order to trade stocks that are extremely volatile with as little research as possible, the following criterion is a good place to start. While additional research is always going to be preferable in the long run, you can find success if you run this scan once a week and pay close attention to the results.

- show stocks where the average day range (50) is above 5%
- and the price is between $10 and $100
- and average volume (30) is greater than 4000000
- and exchange is not Amex
- add column average volume (30)
- add column average day range (50)

This list should ideally return stocks that have moved at least 5 percent every day for the past 50 days. It is important to use a minimum of 50 days, though 75 or 100 will produce even more reliable results overall. Results of this magnitude will show that the stock in question has moved a significant amount over the past few months which means it is likely to continue to do so for the near future.

The second criterion will determine the amount you should be willing to pay per share and can be altered based on your personal preferences.

The third criterion will determine the level of volume that you find acceptable for the given timeframe. The example will look for volume that is greater than four million share within the past month. From there, it will eliminate leverage ETFs from the results which can be eliminated if you are interested in trading ETFs. Finally, the add column will show the list of stocks with the largest amount of volume and the greatest overall amount of movement. Selecting these columns will then rank the results from least to greatest based on the criteria provided.

Monitor regularly: Alternately, you may want to do a daily search to determine the stocks that will experience the greatest range of movement in the coming hours. To do so, you will want to create a new list of stocks every evening to ensure that you will be ready to go when the market opens. This list can then be made up of stocks that have shown a higher volatility in the previous day either in terms of gains or in terms of losses. Adding in volume to this criteria will then help to make sure the results will likely continue to generate the kind of volume that day trading successfully requires. Useful filters for this search include an average volume that is greater than one million and the more you increase the minimum volume the fewer results you'll see.

When using this strategy it is especially important to pick out any stocks that are likely to see major news releases before the next day as these are almost guaranteed to make the price move in a number of random directions before ultimately settling down. As such, it is often best to wait until after the details of the release are known and you can more accurately determine what the response is, though not so long that you miss out on the combination of high volume and high volatility. If you don't already have an earnings calendar bookmarked, the one available for free from Yahoo Finance! is well respected.

Monitor intraday volatility: Another option that is worth considering is doing your researching during the day as a means of determining which stocks are experiencing the greatest overall amount of movement at the moment. A vast majority of trading platforms provide this information in real time so it is easy to keep up to date on the changes that are happening at the moment. For example, if a stock opens at a point down 10 percent from its previous close and stays there you can then assume that there is no one biting on the action that the stock has available.

On the other hand, if the stock starts in a position where it is down 10 percent and then it just keeps dropping then that is a sign it is worth taking a closer look at. You may also find it useful to track stocks that are currently on their way to breaking through the established levels of resistance or support.

Look for bigger moves: In order to find the stocks that are likely to be making big moves sooner than later, without spending all of your free time doing research, you will want to primarily focus on the stocks that are showing a constant state of volatility. This is a great scan to run over the weekend in preparation for the coming week. On the other hand, you can run this scan every night to ensure you know what the differences are likely to be tomorrow. Furthermore, you may instead want to monitor volatility during the day as a means of determining which stocks have seen the most activity during the session in question.

Confirm the chart patterns

Once you have found a few stocks that your scanner indicates are likely to move in the direction you are hoping for, the next step is to double check this fact before you get your hopes up. To do so, you are going to want to review the relative candlestick charts and try and determine the correct entry point based on the point where the first pullback occurred. While many traders will simply buy in at the point where the pullback occurs, this then creates an additional volume spike which pushes the prices even higher. As such, finding the best entry point, in real time, is the key to long-term success.

Pennant: A pennant is a type of indicator that forms when there is significant movement in a given stock, followed by a sudden consolidation period that causes the pennant shape to form from a pair of converging lines. A breakout will then likely occur that goes in the same direction as the previous movement. This typically manifests as extreme movement first, followed by weaker volume from there as the tip of the pennant forms, followed then by more strong growth and even more post-breakout volume.

Cup and handle: The cup and handle pattern looks like the bowl of a cup with the ride side handle. The pattern is u-shaped, charting a series of lows for the stock while the handle also slopes slightly downward. This is a sign that volume is going to remain low overall and that the stock in question should be avoided.

Triangles: Triangles are one of the most frequently seen patterns which tend to occur when the price range converges with the current high, during a period of naturally higher lows. When the convergence is at its peak the price action generates a triangle formation. You will find triangles that are symmetrical, descending and ascending but all three can be traded successfully in the same way. Triangles are going to remain viable trading indicators for differing amounts of time, but you can generally count on them to have two high points and two low swings. When the prices converge, they will then reach an apex and the closer in the timeline it is to this occurring, the tighter the price action ends up being and the closer the price is to experiencing a breakout.

Flags: Unlike triangles, flags can be thought of as a well-defined pause in an ongoing trend that occurs when the price finds itself confined to a small range between a pair of parallel lines. Flags generally only remain intact for a short period of time, lasting a handful of bars, at most. They also don't typically include dramatic price swings the way a common trading range or trend channel likely would. Flags can be either parallel or upward or downward sloping.

Rounded bottom: This pattern tracks a prolonged drop in price that will eventually rebound back to the point where it started. After the rebound occurs a reversal and breakout is likely to occur though it is best avoided as the new trend is likely not going to be strong enough to suit your day trading purposes.

Double top: This pattern is based on a pair of trendlines that are a fair distances apart from one another that track a price through a pair of significant downward movements before returning to the same high point when everything is said and done. After the price breaks through the support line you can expect significant downward movement coming up soon.

Head and shoulders: This indicator is created by three distinct price points, one that is higher than the other two which are on the same line. All three return to the same low point overall. A reverse head and shoulders are also possible where the outlier point is lower than the shoulder points rather than higher. When you see this indicator you can safely assume that a breakout is going to come at the support line to indicate the start of a new downward trend or upward trend in the case of a reverse head and shoulders.

Additional useful things to keep in mind

Be precise on your stops: In order to day trade successfully in the long-term, you need to keep a profit/loss ratio of a minimum of two to one. This means that you are often going to want to set a tight stop that is lower than the first pullback point of the stock that you are following. An ideal target is around 40 cents per share which means that you will want to set your stops 20 cents lower than your target. If you stop is greater than 20 cents you will want to manually end the trade and reassess. This is a useful strategy as it will allow you to generate stops at greater than 20 cents which means you will need to make $1 or more per unit on a trader which is far harder in many cases than you might expect.

You will also find that it is often easier to find success with 40 cents of profit as opposed to holding out for a $1 stop which means you need to make $2 of profit as the day trading market is simply too volatile for this to be useful in most cases. Your goal should then be to balance your overall level of risk across the entire timeframe you are trading in. The easiest way to determine the specific level of risk you are working with is to determine the distance between the entry point and the stop point. If you set a 20 cent stop and want to ensure your total risk amounts to less than $500 then you will still be able to deal in around 2,000 shares at a time.

Best time to trade: While you can successful trade using momentum at any point during the day, you are going to find the greatest degree of success, on average, between 9:30 am and 11:30 am. Even still, if there is an incoming news release then you are still going to want to hold off until you have a general idea of how the market is going to react. If you persist past 11:30 am then you will likely find the best results if you stick to the 5-minute chart exclusively. The 1-minute chart will become much too choppy after 11:30 am to ensure that your stops won't be trigger during normal price movement, making it very difficult to get anything to stick.

Analyze your results: Day trading successfully for any length of time means putting a heavy focus on the statistics behind what you are doing, specifically your overall win/loss ratio as only by monitoring this closely will you be able to regularly ensure that you are moving in the right direction. At the end of each week, your best bet is to determine your overall trading metrics. If you have a full month's worth of subpar metrics you will then want to reconsider your current strategy and see what you can do to improve things for the better overall.

Chapter 5: Tips for success

Choosing the right trades

The best way to ensure that you always choose the right trades is to ensure you never move forward with anything other than a completely measured approach. To guarantee that this is the case you are going to want to start by choosing the type of stocks that most closely align with your personal goals, before ensuring they align with your temperament as well. Additionally, it is important to take into account any external knowledge you might have and focus on stocks where that knowledge might realistically come in handy. Regardless of what types of stocks you ultimately choose to focus on it is important to focus on three primary aspects of a good trade before you make any decisions.

Timeframe: First and foremost, you will always want to trade in the timeframe that you are the most comfortable with, as doing otherwise will cause you to put yourself in situations where you aren't at your best because you are nervous or impatient. To help improve your overall trade percentage as much as possible you will want to stick to the 5-minute charts until you can ensure you are comfortable dealing with the risk that comes from day trading. You will also need to consider the level of micromanaging that you prefer, though your options will be limited if you intend to day trade exclusively.

Tactics: In order to determine the trading methodology that works best for you, it is important to focus on what works for you personally instead of bouncing between strategies and techniques that are popular at the moment. Additionally, it is important to remember that every trader is going to have good weeks and bad and that as long as you can hold onto a trade percentage that is about 60 percent or great then you are well on your way to trading successfully in the long-term.

Making the mistake of constantly switching between tactics is only going to make it more difficult for you to determine if you are moving in the right direction as your data will be skewed in so many different directions. What's worse, changing constantly will make it difficult for you to learn the intricacies of the methodologies you use meaning they will be less effective in even more scenarios.

Key attributes

There are a wide variety of different attributes that all day traders should work to embody to help maximize their potential for success. While you may not be the embodiment of each just yet, with time you can improve on each of them assuming you dedicate the required time to practice each.

Patience: Once you have found a trade that you believe is going to be fruitful, it is important to have the patience required to hold off until just the right time comes along so that when you pull the trigger you know that it is the perfect moment to do so. This is why is always going to be a good idea to determine your entry and exit points beforehand in order to ensure that you can set such things when you are at an optimal mindset. From there, if the trade doesn't perform as expected, you need to have the patience to wait for the right thing to come along.

If you do ultimately decide to chase the potential for profit by altering your entry and exit points on the fly then all you are ultimately going to do is succeed in skewing the overall effectiveness of your plan. After this occurs you will lose, regardless of the short-term outcome as if you profit from bad habits then you will still lose thanks to the positive reinforcement your negative habits received.

Belief: It is important to have belief in the trading plan you created as well as the system that you are using as no plan is going to be 100 percent effective. In fact, a majority of day trading plans can only be considered a success when they are reliably used in the long-term which is another reason that constantly swapping things around is such a bad idea. Don't forget, the right system or plan gives you an edge on the competition and without it, you are essentially just gambling and there are far better ways of doing that than through the stock market. Believe in your system, and yourself and you are sure to see your successful trade percentage increase.

Objectivity: While it can be easy to grow attached to a stock that performs well not just once or twice but on a regular basis time and again, it is important to never grow to rely on any one stock to the point that you are no longer objective when you think of it. Losing sight of this objectivity can cause you to make mistakes like doubling down on a losing proposition, changing your plan mid-trade for no good reason or staying in well past the time the signs told you to get out. The same thing can be said when it comes to listening to outside sources, after a trade is already on the books the only signal you are going to want to follow is your trading plan, everything else is essentially white noise at that point. You need to ensure you can analyze each and every trade based on its own relative merits, if you can manage this then you should be able to trust yourself enough to let everything else take care of itself.

Expectations: It is important to always believe in yourself when it comes to day trading successfully, but your belief should be measured and based on reality as well. Specifically, this means always having a realistic understanding of what your profits are going to be like before you jump into any new trade. Having realistic expectations of this type will ensure that it is much more difficult for you to let your emotions get in the way of making a reliable profit. Keeping your expectations in check means understanding the risk and reward of every trade. Remember, when it comes to day trading, short term trades are more likely to lead to small, safe gains while long term trades are riskier and can end in greater gains.

Motivations: It is important to understand your own motivations in order to be true to yourself and your personal trading style. Likewise, it is important to understand the motivations that different commodity markets have if you hope to trade in them successfully. In order to determine the motivations of your favorite commodities, the first thing you will need to do is consider the major players in the market at the moment. Once you understand that aspect of things you can then watch the commodities themselves as a means of determining how they move and why. Once you are familiar with what is happening at the moment, you can then compare the current movement to the historical movement. When taken as a whole, you can then determine how the moves the major players are making can affect the changing market conditions you are experiencing.

Additional tips

Put your thoughts into action: While it can be difficult to keep everything in your mind at all times, if you never put what you have learned into practice then your skill as a trader is never going to improve. What's worse, you will never be able to turn a profit in a reliable fashion. Once you know what you are doing you will then want to keep track of your trades as soon as you begin, while also not being afraid to bail on a new trade when everything suddenly goes south. After all, a small loss now is always preferable to a potentially much larger loss in the future. Furthermore, it is important to remember that there isn't always going to be a quality trade to make and if this is the case the best way to win in not to play. Don't forget, just because you are a day trader doesn't mean that you need to be trading every minute of every day.

Additionally, it is important to keep in mind that learning all the ins and outs of the market isn't something that can be done through research, it is only something that you can learn by experiencing it for yourself first hand. Additionally, there will be times where the mood of the market and the way the market is moving are going to vary, which means everything that would conventionally be true will be thrown out the window until things right themselves. Ultimately it all comes down to Warren Buffet's number one rule, "the only hard and fast rule is to never lose money." Stick to this rule and you can never go wrong.

Never chase tops or bottoms: While its true that some strategies can be effective when they are used near the top or the bottom of a given trend, these are in the minority, however, and picking tops or bottoms is a risky proposition at best. Unfortunately, it is a common practice for many traders to invest extra money into securities that are either too low or too high, blithely breaking the two percent trading limit rule in the process. This impulse should be avoided at all costs, however, and you should focus on the major inbound move instead. Starting at one side of range-bound markets will lead to better overall results practically all of the time.

Don't try and get even: The market doesn't care about you or anyone, it is only ever concerned about following through on existing patterns. While this is obvious when thought about in a vacuum, many people still attempt to make some trades in an effort to "get even" for previous trades that turned sour right at the worst possible moment. Rather than focusing on these faulty trades, it is far more effective to factor them into your long-term plan and move forward accordingly. Not only will doing so ensure that it is far less likely you will give into your emotions, it will also help to ensure you actually make fewer mistakes down the line as well.

Remember, it is important for you to focus exclusively on the numbers to the exclusion of all else as doing so will allow you to block out any unproductive thoughts you might have regarding things like personal image, magic numbers or breaking even. Just keep reminding yourself that you won't be able to tell if your day has been a failure or a success until the last trade has been completed and don't worry about it until that moment occurs.

Follow the right trends: While existing market trends can easily be a signpost for future movement, they are far from a sure thing. In fact, it is perfectly expected for the market to fluctuate by up to 20 percent on either side of the average at any point and time. This means that if you jump on what you believe to be a solid trend without doing the proper research beforehand then you can easily end up attached to a momentum play that is really going nowhere. Rather, you are going to want to consider each and every trend through the lens of a mixture of timeframes for the best results. If you are fond of short-term trades then daily, hourly and weekly charts are recommended. If you prefer long-term trades then you will want to stick to weekly, daily and monthly charts instead.

Focus, but not too much: Each time you make a trade it is important to keep in mind that you aren't doing so in a vacuum which means trading like you are is only ever going to lead to a steady stream of extremely preventable losses. A better solution would instead be to take more of a macro view of your current trades and act accordingly. Doing so requires that you keep tabs on market leads and also be on the lookout for capital that is like to move in general derivatives. These derivatives are the key in this scenario as they are likely to highlight the many underlying connections between markets that are going to ensure they move as expected. As a general rule, the greater your scope, the more effective you will be.

Avoid strong opinions: While everyone has opinions, the best day traders know that letting them influence your daily trades is only going to lead to a loss of profits. In fact, the only thing you really need to rely on in order to ensure you trade effectively is math, letting anything else into your trading process is only going to get in the way. In order to trade effectively, you need to analyze and observe political events, you can't get caught up in them.

Never average down: While no one ever starts off wanting to average down, it is extremely easy to let it happen if you aren't actively planning against it from the jump. The resources spent holding a weak position will almost always end up being better spent elsewhere as every trade costs you time and weak positions are sure to cost you money as well. Don't forget, every failed trade means that the next one needs to be twice as successful just to ensure you need to brake even, and even more than that to ensure you get ahead and make your trades accordingly.

If your starting trading capital isn't quite where it should be, averaging down can cost you days, if not weeks of trading. If you subsist on short-term trades then you need to be ready to exit as soon as forward momentum slows or, at worst, starts to slip backward. It is really just a question of risk and reward which are naturally part of every trade, though they are rarely ever equal. If a given trade is risky enough to warrant possibly losing ten percent of your daily loss limit then you will want to ensure it will pay out at least twice, if not three times as much to balance out the risk. What's more, it is important to stick to this rule no matter what as letting off of it even once can lead to a slippery slope that will cost you serious cash in the long run.

Choose a trading strategy that meshes with your personality and lifestyle:

Of course, everyone who participates in day trading has a life and it is extremely important that this life is not compromised because of the desire to win money. We have all heard horror stories of people who become obsessed with the stock market and end up throwing their children's tuition down the toilet. Don't let this happen to you!

One of the most important factors for any day trader is to choose a strategy that coincides rather than contrasts that individual's overall personality and character. For example, if you're the type of person who can be patient amidst chaos and you are able to naturally resist the urge to sell and purchase stock through fear or anxiety, then the truth of the matter is that the lifestyle of a traditional stock trader might work better for you than would the life of a day trader. If on the other hand, you find that you are constantly antsy and can't stop thinking about what you're going to do with your money next, then the life of a day trader is right up your ally.

This example is certainly not to try and convince you that day trading isn't for you, but if you are somewhat laidback, then don't you think that day trading is going to cause you anxiety that you're not traditionally used to experiencing? Your trading strategy should coincide with your overall personality, and this requires that you know yourself well enough to choose a trading method that works well for you.

Conclusion

Thank you for making it through to the end of Day Trading: Make Money With These Simple Strategies, the Ultimate Guide to Mastering the Art of Trading, let's hope it was informative and able to provide you with all of the tools you need to achieve your goals, whatever it is that they may be. Just because you've finished this book doesn't mean there is nothing left to learn on the topic, expanding your horizons is the only way to find the mastery you seek. It is important to keep in mind that new day trading strategies are always being developed which means the only way to truly be successful is to commit to becoming a lifelong learner.

Additionally, it is extremely important to keep in mind that while some people are able to see extreme amounts of success in very short periods of time, they are without a doubt the exception rather than the rule. What this means is that it is important to start out your day trading career with measured expectations as you are likely to experience a high degree of losses before you start to get the hang of things, even if you have previous trading experience as day trading is a completely different beast.

While you should most definitely start off with smaller than average trade amounts, you should avoid making the mistake of opening a demo day trading account to practice with as this just won't be able to provide you with the full experience that you need in order to actually improve. This is due to the fact that you will never feel the same way about fake money as you do about the real thing, which makes all of your practice based on a scenario that will simply not transfer over into the real world. As such, the best results will always come from starting small, taking things slow, and only increasing your trade amounts as your confidence increases. Remember, day trading successfully is a marathon, not a sprint, slow and steady wins the race.

Finally, if you found this book useful in any way, a review on Amazon is always appreciated!